USING INTELLIGENCE DATA FOR ENVIRONMENTAL NEEDS

BALANCING NATIONAL INTERESTS

SCOTT PACE

KEVIN M. O'CONNELL

BETH E. LACHMAN

Prepared for the
Community Management Staff

NATIONAL SECURITY RESEARCH DIVISION

RAND

PREFACE

With the end of the cold war, there have been numerous efforts to declassify data and programs that may be able to serve other national objectives in a more open setting. In particular, there has been a growing realization that intelligence community data, such as imagery, may be useful to the conduct of other federal missions such as understanding the environment, managing natural resources, and disaster relief.

Policy, legal, technical, and budgetary considerations all play roles in structuring mutually beneficial cooperation in using intelligence community data for environmental purposes unrelated to intelligence objectives. This report defines these considerations for national policymakers and intelligence community managers and examines alternative structures for cooperation in understanding and protecting the earth's environment.

This report should be of interest to members of the intelligence community, federal agencies with environmental responsibilities, and members of academia and industry who may be affected by the greater availability of intelligence data—particularly imagery—for nontraditional functions.

This work was conducted within the Acquisition and Technology Policy Center of the National Security Research Division of RAND, a non-profit corporation dedicated to policy analysis and research in the public interest.

CONTENTS

FIGURE

TABLES

The end of the cold war and changing national security threats have sparked major debates on the purpose, roles, and functions of the U.S. intelligence community. At the same time, increasing interest in the global environment has raised awareness of how environmental hazards, including natural disasters, can threaten the security of the United States.

The United States has an impressive array of technical systems with which to monitor large areas of the earth, oceans, and atmosphere for national security purposes. These systems have collected sophisticated datasets that span decades, resulting in a unique historical record. These systems also constitute a continuing capability for environmental monitoring, should that be desired.

A key question facing policymakers and intelligence community managers is whether and how to balance routine unclassified environmental activities with traditional intelligence missions and requirements. This question is related to larger debates over the future of the intelligence community as well as narrower objectives of deriving benefits from specific environmental projects using intelligence data. This report discusses the stakeholders, interests, opportunities, and risks for the United States in greater use of intelligence data for environmental purposes by civil agencies, universities, and industry. In particular, the report identifies the following:

- potential risks and benefits for stakeholders
- alternative institutional arrangements that can provide access to intelligence data for environmental purposes
- selection criteria for institutional arrangements.

The current ambiguous state of efforts to use intelligence data for environmental purposes (e.g., support for experiments without commitment to routine use) reflects a lack of consensus on both the value of the data to environmental studies and the value of environmental applications of such data. The attraction of using intelligence data for environmental purposes is fairly simple. The data are already being gathered, or have been gathered, by the U.S. government for one set of purposes, and it may be possible to use the same data for another class of more public purposes. Thus there is the potential to increase public welfare at some relatively low additional cost. Moreover, these data may represent unique observations, in both time and content, that can advance scientific understanding of the environment.

The United States recognizes the importance of environmental issues and problems; however, there are major debates over environmental research generally and the role of governments and markets in dealing with environmental issues. While seemingly remote from immediate scientific questions on the utility of intelligence data, the symbolism of using intelligence data quickly leads to entanglement in larger political questions. Supporting the wider use of intelligence data is seen by some in Congress as approving government spending for environmental research and hence may result in greater government regulation of economic activity. Others argue that better science and environmental monitoring will enable movement away from traditional "command and control" types of regulation to a more flexible regulatory system that will bring environmental benefits at less cost to industry.

Not surprisingly, the most difficult issue is the policy uncertainty stemming from unresolved debates over intelligence community involvement in civil environmental issues, as well as more general debates over intelligence and environmental policy. The next most difficult issue is the lack of civil agency resources (e.g., funds, skilled personnel, facilities, etc.) to support exploration and exploitation of intelligence data for environmental purposes. A new and increasingly important factor in these policy debates is the growing strength of the commercial information industry generally and emergence of a commercial remote-sensing industry in particular. Private industry can benefit from as well as be hurt by environmental applications of intelligence data.

Deciding on the appropriate use of intelligence data and resources for environmental applications requires balancing potential benefits, costs, and risks across multiple interest groups. The benefits and costs of providing intelligence data affect different groups. The group to whom benefits would likely flow are the civil, scientific, and commercial users who have a demand for intelligence data. The group to whom costs would primarily accrue are the government agencies, including their contractors, who may be asked to supply data and access to intelligence systems. The interests of these groups are not clearly separable—for example, the intelligence community may benefit from applications developed by nontraditional users. Alternatively, potential users may incur opportunity costs if the provision of intelligence data crowds out commercial sources.

The case of imagery data may well constitute the predominant policy problem. Other sorts of intelligence data, such as sea ice measurements, will certainly be environmentally useful, but imagery data will likely dominate both the amount of potentially useful data and possible conflicts with private imagery suppliers and other governmental programs. Overseeing the interactions of various interest groups are the President and the Congress, each of whom may have differing views of the relative importance of benefits, costs, and risks.

Selection criteria for choosing how to make intelligence data available for environmental uses emerge from a constellation of relevant stakeholders and national interests. Based on interviews and literature reviews, we see the following factors as being the most crucial:

- Affordability
- Technical merit
- Security risks
- Institutional constraints and preferences

- External acceptance.

Technical merit is the value of conducting specific environmental studies as well as the utility of using intelligence data in a specific study. In scientific studies, value is traditionally established by competitive peer review. These selection criteria were then applied to a range of alternative institutional arrangements:

- A single access center within the intelligence community

- A single access center within the Department of Defense

- A single access center within a civil agency

- A privatized access center

- Maximum data declassification, no single access center

- A network of "virtual centers," no single access center.

The realistic details of these alternatives should be assessed before making recommendations for implementation.

SUMMARY OF RECOMMENDATIONS

- Given the many sensitivities surrounding the use of intelligence data for environmental purposes, specific policy guidance should be provided on what the government will *not* do, as well as what it might do.

- The Administration should promote cooperation on environmental research and management at multiple levels—interagency, international, the private sector, and state and local governments.

- The intelligence community should become a regular participant in interagency environmental fora such as the National Science and Technology Council (NSTC) Committee on Environment and Natural Resources.

- The Administration should seek a greater diversity of funding for civil environmental applications of intelligence data.

- The use of intelligence data for civil environmental applications should become a potential joint mission for the DoD and the intelligence community.

- Greater effort should be expended on declassifying environmental datasets held by the intelligence community and the Department of Defense.

- The intelligence community should initiate a dialog with industry interests that may be affected by more open access to intelligence data for environmental uses.

Presidential direction and bipartisan congressional support are necessary for the sustained use of intelligence data for environmental purposes. Any increased environmental monitoring must not give even the appearance of "domestic spying" or the taking on of law enforcement functions. Political support for even experimental application of intelligence data could quickly vanish.

Some uses of technical intelligence data are more controversial than others and any effort to secure authorizing legislation should focus on applications with the widest possible basis of support. A likely first candidate appears to be natural disaster monitoring, which has a clear public safety mission, past precedents in the use of intelligence data, and potential benefit for state and local communities.

ACKNOWLEDGMENTS

The authors have benefited from numerous discussions with representatives of U.S. government agencies, U.S. industry, academia, and congressional staff. In particular, we would like to thank Central Intelligence Agency officials; Rear Admiral Paul G. Gaffney II and Don Durham, U.S. Navy Meteorology & Oceanography Command; Marylin Pifer, U.S. Department of State; Gary Vest, U.S. Department of Defense; Gene Thorley and Nancy Tosta, U.S. Department of the Interior; Peter Backlund, White House Office of Science and Technology Policy; Lee Tilton, MITRE; Pete Stahl and Robert Morris, KPMG Peat Marwick; and John Schrader and Arnold Kanter of RAND.

We would like to extend a special thanks for the assistance of intelligence community personnel in understanding the range of opportunities and challenges faced in providing support to environmental activities. The final report gained greatly from thoughtful reviews by RAND colleagues Cindi Conlon, James Bonomo, and Susan Resetar. All errors of fact and judgment are those of the authors. Views and recommendations expressed here are not necessarily those of RAND or any of its sponsors.

CENR	Committee on Environment and Natural Resources
CIA	Central Intelligence Agency
CIO	Central Imagery Office
CRG	Civil Requirements Group
DCI	Director Central Intelligence
DIA	Defense Intelligence Agency
DMA	Defense Mapping Agency
DoD	Department of Defense
EOS	Earth Observing System
EPA	Environmental Protection Agency
EROS	Earth Resources Observation System Data Center
ETF	Environmental Task Force
EWG	Environmental Working Group
FEMA	Federal Emergency Management Agency
GATF	Government Applications Task Force
GCOS	Global Climate Observing System
GIS	Geographic Information Systems
GOOS	Global Ocean Observing System
GSD	Ground Separation Distance
GTOS	Global Terrestrial Observing System
IC	Intelligence Community
IGOS	Integrated Global Observing Strategy
IMINT	Imagery Intelligence
JCS	Joint Chiefs of Staff
MASINT	Measurement and Signature Intelligence
MEDEA	A scientific advisory committee (not an acronym)
MOE	Measures of Effectiveness
MTPE	Mission to Planet Earth Program

NASA	National Aeronautics and Space Administration
NAVOCEAN	U.S. Navy Meteorology & Oceanography Command
NETS	National Environmental Technology Strategy
NIMA	National Imagery and Mapping Agency
NOAA	National Oceanic and Atmospheric Administration
NPIC	National Photographic Interpretation Center
NRO	National Reconnaissance Office
NSF	National Science Foundation
NSTC	National Science and Technology Council
OMB	Office of Management and Budget
PDD	Presidential Decision Directive
SIGINT	Signals Intelligence
TFODM	Task Force on Observations and Data Management
USGCCRP	U.S. Global Climate Change Research Program
USGS	U.S. Geological Survey

Chapter One

A CHANGING INTELLIGENCE ENVIRONMENT

INTRODUCTION

The end of the cold war and changing national security threats have sparked major debates on the purpose, roles, and functions of the U.S. intelligence community. At the same time, increasing interest in the global environment has raised awareness of how environmental hazards, including natural disasters, can threaten the security of the United States. Environmental changes from natural and man-made causes can foster conflict over scarce resources, create large-scale human migrations, and destabilize foreign governments. These changes may be rapid, as with nuclear accidents, or gradual, as with global warming. Global environmental monitoring could more effectively manage limited natural resources and environmental problems.

During the cold war, several assumptions dictated how intelligence data were collected, particularly technical collection using expensive ground- and space-based systems. Technical collection of environmental data was assumed to be

- covert
- centralized
- reporting to highest levels of government
- technical state-of-the-art
- targeted on denied areas

1

- looking for strategic threats

- separate from military service or Defense Department control.

Each of these assumptions is being challenged by changing national security needs, expanding open source information, and a more diverse set of intelligence consumers. These assumptions are also largely antithetical to current civil efforts to better understand the earth's environment, such as NASA's Mission to Planet Earth Program (MTPE). The NASA mission is unclassified, with extensive international collaboration and a combination of space-based sensors and ground-based *in situ* measurements. MTPE seeks to be technically state-of-the-art, but unlike traditional intelligence programs, its results are intended for a decentralized, diverse set of users. At first glance, the organizational and cultural gulf between environmental monitoring for civil and intelligence purposes is vast, despite some common technical characteristics. Yet the attraction and real promise of using intelligence data for environmental purposes remains.

The United States has an impressive array of technical systems for monitoring large areas of the earth, oceans, and atmosphere for national security purposes. These systems have collected sophisticated datasets that span decades, and constitute a unique historical record. These systems could be used for environmental monitoring as well as intelligence gathering. The recent Commission on the Roles and Capabilities of the United States Intelligence Community briefly addressed the collection and analysis of environmental information as a role of intelligence. It noted that the intelligence community "monitors international compliance with natural disasters both within the United States and abroad," and that "over the years, the Community's satellite programs have amassed a unique historical collection of ecological data and offer an impressive future capability for environmental monitoring."[1]

The declassification of an early space-based imagery program (CORONA) and availability of previously classified sets of environ-

---

[1] *Preparing for the 21st Century: An Appraisal of U.S. Intelligence,* Report of the Commission on the Roles and Capabilities of the United States Intelligence Community, U.S. Government Printing Office, Washington, D.C., March 1, 1996, p. 26.

mental data (e.g., arctic surveys) have created greater public and scientific community awareness of the potential value of intelligence data for non-intelligence activities. In recent years, the U.S. intelligence community has investigated how it might support scientific, environmental, and other national objectives outside of its traditional domain. The Environmental Task Force, MEDEA,[2] the Government Applications Task Force, the Environmental Working Group of the Gore-Chernomyrdin Commission, and even the use of imagery technologies for improving the early detection of breast cancer are among the more prominent activities.

The intelligence community's efforts have provided unique information while minimizing any effect on traditional intelligence missions from either a resource or security perspective. However, these experimental investigations into potential environmental applications of intelligence data have sometimes been controversial. Some observers of the intelligence community, such as staff members of congressional oversight committees, have been concerned with the legal and policy implications of activities outside of traditional foreign intelligence functions, potential competition for resources, and the benefits (if any) of nontraditional applications of intelligence data to the intelligence community itself. Other observers, such as scientists who have participated in the experimental efforts, have concluded that interactions between the intelligence community and environmental researchers and managers are mutually beneficial and should be encouraged.

POTENTIAL APPLICATIONS

There are numerous examples of how technical intelligence data and derived products can be used in environmental studies, with some types of data more useful than others. Technical intelligence collection is composed of many disciplines and systems, with the major categories being IMINT (imagery intelligence), SIGINT (signals intelligence), and MASINT (measurement and signature intelligence). There is significant functional commonality between commercial and civil remote-sensing activities and IMINT, whereas SIGINT is

---

[2]The term MEDEA is often thought to be an acronym, but it is simply a name.

largely a unique function of the intelligence community. MASINT is a more difficult field to describe; it is defined as

> technically derived intelligence which detects, tracks, identifies, or describes the signatures (distinctive characteristics) of fixed or dynamic target sources . . . MASINT sensors include . . . radar, optical, infrared, acoustic, nuclear, radiation detection, spectroradiometic, and seismic systems as well as gas, liquid, and solid material sampling systems.[3]

If IMINT can be considered similar to the sense of sight, and SIGINT to the sense of sound, then MASINT might be considered to be a combination of touch, taste, and smell—in conjunction with the other senses. MASINT covers many scientific capabilities that could be of environmental interest although developed for national security purposes. As such, it falls between IMINT and SIGINT in terms of overlap with civil and commercial environmental data systems.

Intelligence systems by definition collect foreign intelligence— information on events and activities external to the United States that are of interest to U.S. national security. A natural extension would be to ask how such systems might be used in support of civil agency missions. Sample civil government interests include mapping, natural disasters (e.g., earthquakes, volcanoes, floods, hurricanes, forest fires), search and rescue, natural resource management and preservation (e.g., forests, wetlands, grazing, agriculture, biodiversity), and regulatory violations (e.g., toxic releases, oil spills, waste water discharges). Each of these interests could benefit from current and historical imagery and other types of monitoring data. Moreover, civil agency environmental missions increasingly have international components, such as tracking pollution or coordinating disaster relief. Thus, the use of intelligence data or information derived from intelligence data can support international cooperation.[4]

---

[3]*IC21: Intelligence Community in the 21st Century*, Staff Study, Permanent Select Committee on Intelligence, U.S. House of Representatives, One Hundred Fourth Congress, U.S. Government Printing Office, Washington, D.C., April 9, 1996. p. 149.

[4]Intelligence assets can also be used to create international pressure as, for example, to estimate illegal drug production as an input to the State Department's calculations of foreign aid eligibility.

Basic and applied scientific research can provide a bridge between national security and civil environmental monitoring efforts. To the extent that intelligence data and derived products advance scientific research, all communities can benefit. Uncertainty over the potential scientific value of intelligence datasets has motivated experimental collaborations between traditional environmental scientists and the intelligence community. Environmental scientists have found that some intelligence datasets are unique and valuable scientific resources that are unlikely to be duplicated. An obvious barrier to scientific exploitation, however, is the security classification of the data and sources. Although some scientists have been granted appropriate security clearances, the scientific requirement for open peer review conflicts with the restrictions on handling classified information.

In addition to civil and scientific applications, intelligence data (especially imagery) and derived products may be of commercial value. Commercial applications of airborne and space-based imagery can be found in agriculture, land management, urban planning, oil exploration, pipeline and utility line construction, and construction. The prospect of commercial applications raises concerns in addition to the problem of classification. It can be argued that if government information is available, the government should seek the largest possible public benefit by providing it at the lowest possible cost. Others might argue that the government should not be allowed to compete with private industry and that if data are released, they should be sold at market rates to minimize harm to commercial suppliers.

With the advent of commercial, high-resolution, remote-sensing ventures, IMINT has lost its uniqueness. Historical archives of data, however, continue to be a unique resource that has been barely exploited by civil, scientific, and commercial users, and many new applications can be expected as such archives are opened. These archives might enhance the value of new commercial data sources by providing a basis for historical comparison.

STUDY OBJECTIVES

The final report of the "Commission on the Roles and Capabilities of the U.S. Intelligence Community" concluded that the use of technical capabilities to collect information on environmental problems is legitimate but should not duplicate what civil authorities are able to obtain. The priority given such collection should be weighed against other requirements.[5]

This conclusion leads to a number of questions, such as under what conditions environmental information may be collected for purposes other than foreign intelligence, whether civil capabilities include potential commercial sources, and how priorities for collection should be set.

A key question facing policymakers and intelligence community managers is whether and how to balance routine support of unclassified environmental activities with traditional intelligence missions and requirements. This question is related to larger debates over the future of the intelligence community as well as narrower objectives of ensuring appropriate benefits from specific environmental projects using intelligence data. The following chapters of this report address the stakeholders, interests, opportunities, and risks for the United States in greater use of intelligence data for environmental purposes by civil agencies, universities, and industry. In particular, the report seeks to identify

- potential risks and benefits for stakeholders
- alternative institutional arrangements that can provide access to intelligence data for environmental purposes
- selection criteria for institutional arrangements.

Institutional arrangements (e.g., costs, organizational structure, etc.) were not assessed and the application of selection criteria is only for illustration.

The report discusses data and derived products, not the technology or systems that generated the data or national security requirements for the data. The discussion concentrates on the common policy issues that affect the civil, scientific, commercial, and national security communities.

---

[5] *Preparing for the 21st Century*, 1996.

Chapter Two

STAKEHOLDERS AND NATIONAL INTERESTS

HISTORICAL BACKGROUND

This chapter reviews recent efforts to use intelligence data for environmental purposes. In 1992, the then-Director of Central Intelligence, Robert Gates, established the Environmental Task Force (ETF) at the request of then-Senator Al Gore. The purpose of the ETF was to assess the potential value of classified data to global climate change and other environmental research. For some years preceding, the intelligence community (IC) and environmental researchers had been deadlocked on the subject of declassifying data collected with intelligence systems. When researchers asked if there were any classified data that they could use, the IC would answer that researchers must define their requirements more precisely before they could respond. The ETF engaged some 70 of the nation's leading environmental scientists, conducted background investigations, and provided them with appropriate clearances. These scientists then reviewed large amounts of classified data and other information to see if a unique perspective could be brought to bear on environmental research questions that could not be addressed otherwise. The ETF thus focused on questions of utility, importance, and uniqueness in the potential of intelligence data to contribute to environmental research.

Through analyses, pilot projects, and experiments, the ETF determined that useful and unique environmental measurements could be extracted from classified data sets and information derived from classified space and ground systems. The ETF also advanced the concept of unclassified derived products (primarily graphical) to facilitate access to limited, specific types of information from intelligence data.

In 1994, the ETF was transitioned into a continuing IC-funded Environmental Program. The objective of this program is to determine what information can be routinely used from the intelligence community without prejudicing intelligence missions. One part of the program consists of 57 scientists from the ETF who serve as a scientific advisory committee known as MEDEA. This committee meets regularly and supports the IC through analyses, evaluation of proposed advanced systems, and identification of new applications that support intelligence missions.

A 1995 MEDEA special report provides insight into the types of assessments conducted by the committee, using examples drawn from ocean data.[1] The Naval Meteorology and Oceanography Command uses data measurements of marine gravitational and magnetic fields, seafloor bathymetry and sediment properties, and ocean characteristics such as salinity and vertical temperature profiles.[2] Ships, aircraft, submarines, and satellites collected these data from most of the world's oceans in the decades of the cold war. The 1993 ETF final report dealt largely with space-based collection systems, with some attention to Navy systems and databases.

Like the ETF report, the MEDEA special report concluded that classified Naval data could make unique, important contributions to environmental research. MEDEA recommended that the Navy consider prompt declassification of high-priority datasets, such as marine gravity, geomagnetics, submarine ice keel depth acoustic data, high-resolution marine bathymetry, and Geosat satellite altimetry.[3] The selection of these datasets was based on the uniqueness of the Navy data, the near-impossibility of replication by a civil agency or even an

---

[1] *Scientific Utility of Naval Environmental Data*, a MEDEA Special Task Force Report, Washington, D.C., June 1995.

[2] Ibid., p. 1.

[3] Submarine ice keel depth refers to the varying lengths of submerged ice, usually in the Arctic, which can prevent a submarine vessel from surfacing. Geosat satellite altimetry refers to altimetry data taken from Geosat satellites that can be used to measure variations in the earth's gravitational field.

international group of civil agencies (partly because of the high cost of the submarine and satellite platforms needed for data gathering), and their value to scientific research.

The ETF included participation from agencies with environmental missions or interests, including the Departments of Defense, Commerce, Interior, and Energy, as well as the National Aeronautics and Space Administration (NASA) and others. As an outgrowth of the ETF, a Government Applications Task Force (GATF) was formed with the intelligence community and eight civil federal agencies (the Departments of Defense, Interior, Energy, Agriculture, and Transportation/U.S. Coast Guard, Commerce/National Oceanic and Atmospheric Agency (NOAA), the Federal Emergency Management Agency, and the Environmental Protection Agency). The GATF found that classified intelligence data could provide unique contributions and benefit environmental work by civil agencies.

A prominent area of international cooperation supported by the Environmental Program is the Gore-Chernomyrdin Commission. An Environmental Working Group (EWG) was created by a Joint Statement of Vice President Gore and Prime Minister Chernomyrdin at their June 1995 Moscow meeting. The EWG examines approaches to the uses of space-based, airborne, oceanographic, and *in situ* products from national security collection systems for environmental purposes. The EWG Russian co-chair is Minister V. I. Danilov-Danilyan and the American co-chair is Dr. James Baker, who heads the National Oceanic and Atmospheric Administration. Current agreed-upon projects include:

- Global environmental disaster monitoring
- Arctic climatology and navy-to-navy oceanography cooperation
- Environmental impact of oil and gas activities in arctic and sub-arctic regions
- Land use/forestry studies
- Military base and radioactive facility clean-up
- Earthquake prediction.

At the same time that environmental activities were starting to use classified data, the U.S. government began declassifying older intelli-

gence satellite imagery. In 1995, the earliest U.S. reconnaissance
satellite programs—CORONA, ARGON, and LANYARD—were declassified by Executive Order.[4] Some 17,000 cans of original photographic negatives, recovered from space during 1960–1972, were
transferred to the National Archives in College Park, Maryland, and
the U.S. Geological Survey Earth Resources Observation System
(EROS) Data Center in Sioux Falls, South Dakota, where they are to
be made available to the public. Some reduced-resolution images
can be seen today on the Internet via the USGS' World Wide Web
site.[5] Interest in the declassified images has come primarily from
historians, government officials, and retirees who used to work on
the early satellite programs.[6]

Environmental researchers welcomed the declassification of older
satellite imagery as a low-cost source of historical data on snowfall
variations, deforestation, and changing lake and stream patterns.[7] In
particular, imagery was now available for large areas of the Eurasian
land mass to which access had traditionally been denied to Western
scientists. There were, however, concerns in the emerging commercial remote-sensing industry that the release of high-resolution
(about 2-meter ground separation distance [GSD]) imagery could be
a source of competition. These concerns were partially allayed by
the fact that the data released represented a fixed amount and did
not include access to currently operating systems. Additionally, operating licenses had been granted for higher-resolution commercial
systems and the old government images could conceivably spur interest in access to more timely commercial images.

RECENT POLICY AND BUDGET DECISIONS

Efforts to make greater use of intelligence data for environmental research are still experimental and face resistance for a variety of rea-

---

[4]*Release of Imagery Acquired by Space-Based National Intelligence Reconnaissance Systems*, Executive Order 12951, Washington, D.C., February 22, 1995.

[5]WWW site URL is http://edcwww.cr.usgs.gov/dclass/dclass.html

[6]"NRO Images Available to the Public, But Early Use is Light," *Space Business News*, May 15, 1996, p. 8.

[7]"The Art and Science of Photoreconnaissance," Dino A. Brugioni, *Scientific American*, March 1996, pp. 78–85.

sons. At senior policy levels, save for the strong interest of Vice President Gore, environmental issues are not considered a priority in the intelligence community. The most recent presidential statement of national intelligence priorities, Presidential Decision Directive (PDD) 35, outlines a tiered structure of prioritized needs and collection and analysis guidance.[8] Environmental issues are not a priority in themselves, but as they affect intelligence objectives. Scientific research *per se* is, naturally, not an intelligence need.

It has been difficult to obtain funds to support assessments of intelligence data for environmental purposes. The IC has sought to move from its wholly classified Environmental Program to one that is balanced with (and partially funded by) U.S. civil agencies. In the fall of 1995, a budget transition strategy was proposed to the interagency Civil Requirements Group (CRG), which consisted of NASA, NOAA, the National Science Foundation (NSF), the U.S. Geological Survey (USGS), and the Environmental Protection Agency (EPA), as well as the intelligence community. A commitment of $4.6 million per year was sought from the civil agencies starting in FY97 for activities supporting their missions and responsibilities (including a MEDEA contribution of $1 million per year). In comparison, the intelligence community's Environmental Program was authorized at $18 million in FY97.

The bulk of civil budget responsibility was sought from five agencies—NASA, NOAA, NSF, USGS, and the U.S. Department of Agriculture. Additional contributions were sought from the U.S. Coast Guard, EPA, and the Federal Emergency Management Agency (FEMA). Other agencies, such as the Army Corps of Engineers and the Department of Energy, might participate as well, but the level of CRG activities was expected to be low, so no contributions were sought. This approach did not work, however; the FY97 budget proved to be tighter than expected, particularly in the discretionary accounts where the civil agencies are located in the federal budget. No civil agencies came forward to make the requested contributions.

At the instigation of the Vice President, the Secretary of the Interior and the Office of Management and Budget (OMB) included $5

---

[8]*IC21*, 1996, p. 88. PDD 35 was signed by President Clinton on March 5, 1995.

million in the FY97 budget request for the U.S. Geological Survey. This money was slated for "infrastructure upgrades for environmental programs and mapping activities using data from the intelligence community," as well as contributing support to MEDEA scientists for environmental applications.[9] The USGS and the intelligence community have long cooperated in the development of maps, and thus present a precedent for this request by the congressional authorization and appropriation committees for the Department of the Interior. In the near term, funding is likely to be available for continuing exploration of civil environmental applications of classified data. The long-term feasibility and desirability of working through the Department of the Interior is still in doubt, however, because the costs are being placed in one civil agency while the potential benefits are spread more widely.

The problem of budgeting for environmental uses of intelligence data highlights a basic reality: funding sources are different from the places where benefits are expected to occur. Known costs have to be balanced against uncertain benefits accruing outside of the organizations that control the data in question. As a result, no single agency or group is in a position to make a clear determination of the appropriate balancing between different national interests. These interests and stakeholders are discussed below.

NATIONAL INTERESTS AND STAKEHOLDERS

The potential use of intelligence data for environmental purposes in both the public and private sectors raises issues that cut across numerous organizations and interests. The wide range of issues and interests found in different organizations determine how differing policy proposals might be received. A number of government and industry officials were interviewed during the course of this study, and while we have attempted to convey their views accurately, the following interpretations do not represent official positions.

---

[9] *The Interior Budget in Brief for FY97*, U.S. Geological Survey—Bureau Summary, U.S. Government Printing Office, Washington, D.C., March 1996, p. 70.

Administration Viewpoints

Stemming from his efforts in the Senate, Vice President Al Gore has continued to support the use of intelligence data for environmental research. These uses remain experimental and exploratory, however, and are not a routine part of Administration or agency activities. At high policy levels, there is interest in using intelligence data combined with wariness over how such use will impact agency budgets and missions. Within the National Security Council and the intelligence community's own National Intelligence Council, the role of environmental concerns in national security strategy (e.g., the link between environmental degradation and regional conflict) continues to be debated.[10] Information about the environment is usually seen as a factor that may affect other national interests, not something to be sought for its own sake.

The President coordinates science and technology policies across the federal government through the National Science and Technology Council (NSTC), a cabinet-level council. An important objective of the NSTC is to establish clear national goals for federal science and technology investments. Within the NSTC, the Committee on Environment and Natural Resources (CENR) is one of nine committees that cover a broad area of federal research and development. The CENR coordinates programs among 12 federal agencies and attempts to focus environmental and natural resources R&D on those questions that most directly impact health and the economy. CENR goals include enhancing environmental quality and improving the information available for environmental policymaking. In this process, earth observation and monitoring are seen as "a critical component of environmental and natural resources research that is aimed at advancing scientific understanding and developing predictive assessment capabilities, products, and services."[11]

---

[10]"American Diplomacy and the Global Environmental Challenges of the 21st Century," Secretary of State Warren Christopher, Palo Alto, California, April 9, 1996.

[11]*Preparing for the Future Through Science and Technology: An Agenda for Environmental and Natural Resource Research*, National Science and Technology Council, Committee on Environment and Natural Resources, Washington, D.C., March 1995, pp. 4–7.

In their 1995 strategic planning document, the CENR identified environmental observations and data management "for enhanced emphasis in the research and budget planning cycles of the CENR federal agencies with environment and natural resources research."[12] Specifically, they emphasized the need for accurate and efficient measurements and that the data be made easily available to all stakeholders. The CENR has a subcommittee, called the Task Force on Observations and Data Management (TFODM), which is trying to inventory and integrate the nation's observation and data system requirements and capabilities. They are developing a more comprehensive global and national observation and monitoring system and a complementary data management system to make sure that environmental and natural resource management information is accessible.

The CENR TFODM serves as the U.S. focal point for international global observing systems such as the Global Climate Observing System (GCOS), the Global Terrestrial Observing System (GTOS), and the Global Ocean Observing System (GOOS). The TFODM includes designated representatives from almost all federal agencies involved in any type of collection or use of environmental data. NASA, NOAA, EPA, and NSF are the most active participants; the IC has not been involved. The CENR TFODM is attempting to

- link local-scale data collection efforts with regional- and global-scale efforts

- link remote-sensing data from satellite with *in situ* measurements

- link socioeconomic data with data on the natural environment

- make the agency environmental data and information available in useful form to the public, educators, policymakers, business activities, and researchers.[13]

For example, the TFODM has been working on a U.S. concept for an Integrated Global Observing Strategy (IGOS) to integrate existing and

---

[12]Ibid., p. viii.

[13]Ibid., pp. 4–8.

new observing capabilities into a coherent system. It takes into account joint international efforts, such as GCOS, GTOS, and GOOS, and U.S. federal agency efforts. This integration effort illustrates how the CENR is trying to reduce duplication of effort and leverage scarce resources in the face of declining federal budgets in such areas. The effort will not be complete until an appropriate role for the intelligence community is decided.

The CENR also has a subcommittee on environmental technologies and an Environmental Monitoring Team, which both recognize the importance of environmental monitoring and data management.[14] For example, one of the goals of the National Environmental Technology Strategy (NETS) is to "Improve the nation's environmental monitoring data and information systems substantially over the next five years . . ."[15] The Environmental Monitoring Team is developing a framework for integrating the nation's environmental monitoring and research networks and programs.

Clearly, the Administration has an interest in environmental monitoring and data and improving the integration of such information. Past MEDEA efforts have identified monitoring of specified "global fiducial" environmental characteristics as an area in which historical intelligence data and current systems could make unique and valuable contributions. However, a routine role for intelligence data in environmental research and monitoring has yet to be defined. As a result, efforts to operationalize the use of intelligence data in civil environmental work have been slow and spotty.

Federal Agency Viewpoints

Within U.S. government agencies, attitudes toward using intelligence data for environmental purposes depend on the importance of environmental issues to those agencies and whether the agencies are able to acquire their own data or are dependent on outside sources.

---

[14]The CENR estimated that the combined federal environmental monitoring and research budget totaled more than $6 billion in FY95; some $500 million of this was for major federal environmental monitoring networks.

[15]*Bridge to a Sustainable Future: National Environmental Technology Strategy,* U.S. Government Printing Office, Washington, D.C., April 1995, p. 62.

A willingness to use intelligence data can depend on what alternatives are available. A simplistic, but useful, distinction can be made between organizations that have large-system technical capabilities (e.g., independent space systems) and those that do not. Both may be able to process intelligence data, such as remote-sensing images, and "add value" in their use of such data.

Table 1 lists government organizations with potential interests in using intelligence data for environmental applications, categorized by whether they can field space systems. Agencies are listed in order of their ability to use unprocessed intelligence data, beginning with those with internal analytical assessment skills to those that require others to process data into finished products.

Within the Department of Defense, the Central Imagery Office (CIO) is the focal point for DoD imagery activities and is jointly staffed by DoD and Central Intelligence Agency (CIA) personnel. The CIO does not, however, include the CIA's National Photographic Interpretation Center (NPIC) or the National Reconnaissance Office (NRO, responsible for space intelligence systems). In December 1995, the Director, Central Intelligence (DCI), Secretary of Defense, and the Chairman of the Joint Chiefs of Staff proposed the estab-

Table 1

**Potential U.S. Government Users of Intelligence Data
for Environmental Purposes**

Space Capabilities	Nonspace Capabilities
Department of Defense	Department of Defense
Intelligence community	Intelligence community
NASA	NASA
NOAA	NOAA
	Department of the Interior
	Department of Agriculture
	EPA
	FEMA
	U.S. Army Corps of Engineers
	Department of Transportation
	Department of State
	National Science Foundation

lishment of a National Imagery and Mapping Agency (NIMA) that would include NPIC and the Defense Mapping Agency (DMA) as well as the CIO. NIMA would be responsible for all aspects of imagery and would be designated a "combat support agency" responsible to the Chairman of the JCS for joint war-fighting.[16]

The debate over how the United States can best meet its national security needs for imagery intelligence is broad and complex. The NIMA proposal in particular has attracted criticism that the benefits of centralization are not worth the risk of national intelligence requirements being given less priority than military needs in an organization reporting to the Joint Staff.[17] The issue of national versus military intelligence needs is reflected in differing views on using intelligence in environmental applications. Some contend that such usage should be prioritized with other civil, national requirements and not compete with military requirements. Others see military interactions with environmental researchers (e.g., the U.S. Navy's Meteorology & Oceanography Command) as so beneficial that they should be pursued regardless of civil priorities. Finally, there are those who see environmental uses of intelligence data as a minor factor in allocating resources, so that any debate is largely political without significant operational impacts.

The Department of Defense has an Environmental Security Office that manages its environmental program. It is structured around issues such as environmental compliance, pollution prevention, conservation, and clean-up. As Secretary of Defense William J. Perry stated, DoD

---

[16]NIMA was formally established on October 1, 1996 as a result of the National Imagery and Mapping Agency Act of 1996. NIMA is part of the U.S. intelligence community and incorporates the Defense Mapping Agency, the Central Imagery Office, and the Defense Dissemination Program Office; the mission and functions of the CIA's National Photographic Interpretation Center; and the imagery exploitation, dissemination, and processing elements of the Defense Intelligence Agency, National Reconnaissance Office, and Defense Airborne Reconnaissance Office.

[17]There has been less discussion of consolidating SIGINT activities and balancing national and military needs, for several reasons. SIGINT activities are already highly centralized, technically specialized, and even more heavily classified than IMINT. In addition, there are few dual-use applications of SIGINT compared to IMINT and thus few incentives to create alternative institutions to exploit SIGINT data.

has an aggressive environmental program for several important reasons. First, because environmental responsibility must be an inte-
gral part of any large organization with industrial activities, and
DoD is the nation's largest. Second, because many of the
Department's practices over the years, while acceptable and legal at
the time, have created an extensive environmental clean-up task.
Third, because DoD must comply with the same state and federal
environmental statutes, regulations and policies as the rest of the
nation.

Finally, DoD has an aggressive environmental program because it is
critical to the defense mission. Why? Because it protects the quality
of life of our forces and their families from environmental health
and safety hazards where they live and work.[18]

As part of the DoD effort, the Principal Assistant Deputy Under
Secretary of Defense (Environmental Security), Gary Vest, leads a
small program that seeks to both coordinate DoD environmental activities more effectively and promote international military-to-
military environmental cooperation, especially with the former
Soviet Union. Policy debates seem to be less important in
comparison to an ethic of "just do it" in establishing model programs
and demonstrations.

Under the Environmental Working Group of the Gore-Chernomyrdin
Commission, the United States and Russia exchanged intelligence
data on selected military bases to aid environmental assessment and
clean-up, as well as information on arctic climatology. The DoD
Environmental Security Office has been an active participant in these
efforts, but in April 1996 DoD moved its cooperative program from
the Gore-Chernomyrdin Commission to a bilateral agreement with
the Russian Ministry of Defense.[19] The primary motivation for the
move seemed to be perceived bureaucratic and funding impedi-
ments in using the Commission rather than any Administration dis-
agreement over the desirability of the activity itself. Intelligence data
continue to be used, but the focus is on leveraging available re-

---

[18] *TODAY: America's Forces Protect the Environment,* DoD Legacy Resource
Management Program, project magazine, Washington, D.C., 1995, p. 5.

[19] "Memorandum Between the Department of Defense of the United States of America
and the Ministry of Defense of the Russian Federation on Cooperation in
Environmental Protection Issues," Moscow, Russia, June 30, 1995.

sources for existing missions rather than on seeking dedicated resources for new exploitations of intelligence data.

Outside of the national security community, NASA and the
Department of Commerce's NOAA can deploy and operate space-
based remote-sensing systems. NOAA operates several weather
satellites in polar and geosynchronous orbit, and NASA is pursuing
"Mission to Planet Earth" (MTPE) as part of the interagency U.S.
Global Climate Change Research Program (USGCCRP). Mission to
Planet Earth is expected to constitute about 70 percent of the total
USGCCRP, with major elements being the space-based Earth
Observing System (EOS) and ground-based data systems.[20] The
USGCCRP is, in turn, expected to contribute to international global
environmental observations as part of an Integrated Global
Observing Strategy.

Although NASA and NOAA agencies have long had cooperative relations with the intelligence community, intelligence data have not
been a routine requirement for pursuing environment-related operations. Budget pressures have prompted interest in using data from
foreign, international, and even classified sources. Data from U.S.
intelligence systems have the advantage of already existing within
the U.S. government, but the barriers to using the data appear
formidable to NASA and NOAA. As will be discussed in the next
chapter, major uncertainties lie with the scientific utility of the data
and the burden of classification. Because peer review is considered
essential to scientific research, data not available for open scrutiny
and independent verification are seen as effectively useless.

A number of U.S. government agencies support sophisticated data
processing (including imagery) functions without operating space
systems as well. The analytical arms of the intelligence community,
including the CIA and the Defense Intelligence Agency (DIA), conduct research that requires environmental data from classified and
unclassified sources. Within the Department of the Interior, the U.S.
Geological Survey has used intelligence data for mapping, geodesy,
and other purposes for years. USGS has both a sophisticated data-

---

[20] *Omnibus Civilian Science Authorization Act of 1996,* Committee on Science Report
Together with Dissenting Views, U.S. House of Representatives, One Hundred Fourth
Congress, Report 104-550, Washington, D.C., May 1, 1996, p. 50.

handling capability and requisite security measures to deal with intelligence data. The Department of Agriculture uses aerial and satellite photography to create maps and statistical reports in support of its programs. The Foreign Agriculture Service may use classified data for crop yield predictions and disaster monitoring. The National Science Foundation does not have its own internal scientific capabilities, but instead supports diverse university and industry scientists who conduct environmental research. As mentioned earlier, the NSF contributes to the ambitious interagency Global Climate Change Research Program.

The organizations mentioned above—the CIA and DIA, the Departments of the Interior and Agriculture, and the National Science Foundation—have varying degrees of experience with using intelligence data for environmental purposes. In the intelligence community, handling intelligence data is routine, but environmental issues are not central to its mission. In the case of Interior and Agriculture, environmental data are central to their missions and intelligence data have been routinely used albeit in limited areas. In the case of NSF, environmental data are central to some NSF-supported research, but classification barriers have constrained the use of intelligence data. Members of these organizations tend to reflect the missions of the agencies. Staff at Interior and Agriculture are open to the use of intelligence data, and classification procedures, although a burden, do not constitute a problem. Intelligence analysts, while interested in and supportive of environmental applications of classified data, do not generally see the pursuit of such applications as part of their jobs.

Figure 1 is a simple categorization of potentially interested agencies by their experience with intelligence data and the importance of environmental data to agency missions. There is no agency highly experienced with intelligence data that faces environmental concerns as an important main mission. On the other hand, there are agencies who have one of these attributes and are moving toward acquiring the other. The national security community as a whole is showing more interest in environmental concerns. Some civil environmental agencies are showing increasing interest in intelligence data and are attempting to evaluate the potential benefits, costs, and risks involved.

RAND*MR799-1*

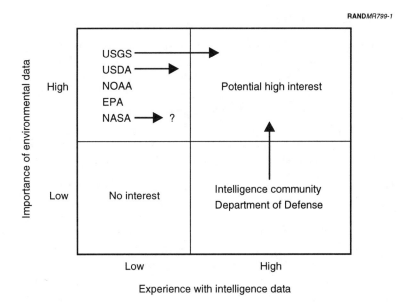

Figure 1—No Clear, Single Agency Sponsor

Finally, there are those agencies which may become consumers of intelligence data for environmental purposes but which lack large-scale technical capabilities, personnel, and budgets to process the data. Their use of intelligence data will depend largely on how beneficial, costly, and difficult it is in comparison with open or commercial sources. Typical agencies include the Environmental Protection Agency, the Federal Emergency Management Administration, the U.S. Army Corps of Engineers, the U.S. Coast Guard, multiple bureaus within the Department of the Interior, and the Department of State (in areas of scientific and environmental cooperation). While interested in the potential utility of intelligence data, agency staff are likely to see unclassified data sources as more convenient to use. Older forms of intelligence data, for example, can be difficult to use because of both security restrictions and outdated storage formats.

Congressional Viewpoints

Congress has not decided whether or to what extent intelligence data should be used for civil environmental purposes. Debates over the future of the intelligence community have emphasized major organizational and budgetary issues such as relations with the military services and the utility of new technologies in lowering the cost of intelligence systems.[21] As might be expected, these debates have been largely within the congressional intelligence committees, rather than in the DoD oversight or appropriations committees.

Using intelligence data in civil environmental applications has not been a major funding issue, and thus congressional staff views tend to be shaped by partisan and philosophical concerns. Partisan feelings since the 104th Congress are strong in the House, and Vice President Gore's support for environmental applications can evoke opposition on that basis alone. In general, Democratic staff tend to be sympathetic to finding new applications for intelligence data whereas Republican staff prefer that the intelligence community focus on its traditional missions.

The increasingly tight budget environment has stimulated interest from other congressional committees in using data and systems. For example, the House Science Committee has been concerned about the costs of global climate change research, especially NASA's MTPE. In 1996, the Committee delayed the schedules of two major MTPE satellites (known as PM-1 and Chem-1) to "give NASA time to survey and assess . . . the Department of Defense's airborne and space-based sensor program to avoid duplication and waste of taxpayer dollars."[22] In contrast to the intelligence committees, this interest came from the Republican members and staff.

At the moment, Congress seems to be following a path of "benign neglect" while experiments and demonstrations such as MEDEA proceed. Neither the intelligence committees or oversight committees for agencies with environmental missions have firm views on the value of these efforts. Such issues as the creation of a National Imagery and Mapping Agency (established October 1, 1996), the de-

---

[21] *IC21*, 1996, pp. 108–110.

[22] *Omnibus Civilian Science Authorization Act of 1996.*

gree and necessity of intelligence data classification, and the availability of commercial data sources will likely drive future congressional action rather than the technical merits of intelligence data in environmental uses. Nonetheless, legislation defining the purposes and constraints of environmental or other non-intelligence uses will be a necessity if the practice is to become routine. Such legislation will need the support of both intelligence and civil agency oversight committees if it is to become law.

U.S. Industry and International Viewpoints

The acquisition of space-based remote-sensing and oceanographic data, the most common forms of environmentally significant intelligence data, has traditionally been dominated by the government. In recent years, a commercial space remote-sensing industry has emerged as a result of presidential and congressional encouragement.[23] While the global market for remote-sensing data is currently small, the domestic and international implications of commercially driven growth have caused much discussion.[24] As a result, U.S. industry viewpoints will likely play a significant role in U.S. policy on the use of intelligence data for environmental purposes as well—even though only a portion of such data is imagery.

U.S. industry views on the use of intelligence data vary by sector. Firms that supply intelligence systems and support services do not see environmental applications as a growth sector for the government, but learning more about such applications may benefit commercial markets, which are growing. The most vocal firms on environmental uses of intelligence data are those with ventures in the new field of commercial high-resolution remote sensing, in which intelligence imagery may be a complement or substitute good. There is little debate over datasets that are widely seen as unique, e.g., information on the deep ocean or arctic climatology.

---

[23] *Policy on Foreign Access to Remote Sensing Space Capabilities,* Fact Sheet, U.S. Department of Commerce, March 10, 1994.

[24] *New Satellite Images for Sale, the Opportunities and Risks Ahead,* Vipin Gupta, Lawrence Livermore National Laboratory, Center for Security and Technology Studies, CSTS-47-94, Livermore, California, September 28, 1994.

The most visible high-resolution commercial remote-sensing firms are Space Imaging (which is a venture of Lockheed Martin), OrbView (which is part of Orbital Sciences), and EarthWatch (in which Ball Aerospace is a major partner). EOSAT, the firm that markets LANDSAT remote sensing data, is also part of Lockheed Martin.[25] Each firm is pursuing business strategies in terms of space system architectures, financing, and marketing strategies.[26] The firms are generally united in opposition to the release of intelligence data for civil environmental purposes. This opposition stems from several, interrelated concerns. First, imagery from intelligence systems may well compete and the government will charge only a nominal fee or no fee at all. Second, cooperative efforts between the intelligence community and foreign nations may compete with firms for investment capital—that is, a foreign country will choose to work with the U.S. government rather than with a private U.S. company. Third, without clear boundaries and definitions on what types of intelligence data will be released and for what purposes, potential investors worry about the stability of U.S. policy and avoid this market even without adverse U.S. government actions.

While some firms would not like to see the declassification and release of any intelligence imagery, even historical archives, others support the release of older material as potentially helpful under limited conditions. For example, the release of old intelligence images could stimulate sales of more current images from commercial systems. Industry representatives feel that it is important that such releases be limited to discontinued programs (such as CORONA), and that the quality of released images should be no better than that for which the government is willing to grant commercial operating licenses. The argument is that if the government limits the resolution of commercial remote-sensing systems, it should not be allowed to release images with superior resolution. The Commerce Department, which grants commercial remote-sensing operating licenses, has generally supported industry concerns.

---

[25]Lockheed Martin has announced that it intends to purchase the Hughes Aircraft interest in EOSAT. Lockheed Martin Missiles & Space Press Release 96-32, Sunnyvale, California, June 7, 1996.

[26]*Emerging Markets of the Information Age: A Case Study in Remote Sensing Data and Technology*, C. B. Gabbard, K. O'Connell, G. Park, and P. J. E. Stan, RAND, DB-176-CIRA, 1996.

Several foreign countries have or are developing high-resolution remote-sensing systems for military and commercial purposes (e.g.,
Russia, France, Israel, India, China, Japan, and Korea). Virtually all of
them have direct government involvement and support and serve
multiple purposes. Russia and the United States are largely unique
in terms of having sophisticated space intelligence capabilities and
extensive archives of historical intelligence data. They have done the
most experimenting with potential environmental applications in
internal and bilateral cooperative efforts. No country outside the
United States has fully commercial remote-sensing ventures, so less
attention has been given to the issue of potential government competition with the private sector. On the other hand, foreign countries
are keenly aware of the potential competitive opportunity and threat
posed by U.S. firms.

Foreign governments tend not to have clear or rigid boundaries in
their views on using intelligence data. Aside from the enduring issue
of classification, it does not matter very much if intelligence data
gathered for military purposes also find environmental applications.
The budget limits faced by the United States are even more severe in
other countries considering investments in space systems. Thus, any
ability to find multiple users for the same data, and thus multiple
sources of support, is welcomed. Environmental applications may
be sought out by foreign governments to bolster support for building
intelligence capabilities.

KEY MOTIVATIONS AND UNCERTAINTIES

The current ambiguous status of applying intelligence data for environmental purposes—i.e., support for experiments without commitment to routine use—reflects a lack of consensus on both the
value of the data to environmental studies and the value of environmental applications of such data. The attraction of using intelligence
data for environmental purposes is straightforward. The data are already being gathered, or have been gathered in the past, by the U.S.
government, and it may be possible to use the same data for another
class of public purposes. There is the potential to increase the public
welfare at a relatively low public cost.

Of course, uncertainties in environmental applications can create
unexpected costs and lower the benefits in using intelligence data.

Since the organizations who might use the data are not identical with the ones tasked with gathering, maintaining, and paying for the data, the views of various potential stakeholders can be understood in terms of how uncertainties might affect them individually. Will release of the data compromise other intelligence missions? Will support of environmental applications create reciprocal benefits for the intelligence community? Will wider availability of intelligence imagery harm commercial remote-sensing ventures? Most important, are there civil agencies that are willing to pay (and how much) for access to specific kinds of intelligence data?

The wide range of potential benefits of using intelligence data for environmental work should be contrasted with the narrow range of who pays the costs (i.e., the national security community) and what organizations may be harmed (i.e., commercial firms). Finding a mechanism to more nearly balance potential benefits, costs, and risks—in a period of declining federal budgets—is the chief challenge to any transition from current experimental efforts to more routine exploitation. At a policy level, there is the question of whether intelligence data should be made available for environmental uses at all, and if so, under what conditions. Upon implementation, there is the question of allocating organizational and funding responsibilities, ensuring intelligence data are protected appropriately, and that data are not misused. The numerous difficult trade-offs will be discussed in the next chapter.

Chapter Three

BENEFITS, COSTS, AND RISKS

Two primary groups need to understand the benefits, costs, and risks of using intelligence data for civil environmental applications. The first are the civil, scientific, and commercial interests who may create a demand for intelligence data. The second are the national security interests (primarily government agencies and their contractors) who may be asked to supply data and access to intelligence systems. Overseeing the interactions of these two groups are the President and the Congress, each of whom will be called upon to set the boundaries and terms of the market, if any, for intelligence data outside of the national security community.

The diverse interests found in both the "supply" and "demand" groups are reflected in Executive Branch actions such as Presidential Decision Directives and Executive Orders. At the same time, Congress has a vital role in shaping agency priorities through its use of legislation and appropriations. Congressional judgments of benefits, costs, and risks will depend on the views of "supply" and "demand" groups, but can be independent of Administration policy. To date, however, Congress has not looked at the issues involved in environmental uses of intelligence data.

CIVIL/SCIENTIFIC/COMMERCIAL INTERESTS

At present, intelligence data are not a significant source for civil environmental research. As a result of the Environmental Task Force and the continuing work of MEDEA, however, some leading environmental scientists believe that intelligence data and systems are potentially beneficial to their work. Intelligence data can constitute a unique resource that is unlikely to be replicated. In other cases, access to intelligence systems can provide unique capabilities for environmental work that are unlikely to be otherwise available. An important potential benefit of unique data and systems is that they may yield information on new phenomena, enhanced monitoring coverage (e.g., in range and repeatability), and provide flexibility for covering unexpected events (e.g., volcano eruptions). For example, submarines have carried oceanographers under the arctic ice, ocean sound monitoring systems have tracked whales, and space remote-sensing systems have identified forest fires in remote regions.

Intelligence data and systems can aid civil and commercial environmental monitoring systems, especially in remote sensing from air and space. Intelligence information can verify or validate the functioning of more open systems, cue the systems to potentially productive areas to examine, and provide "lessons learned" for developing future environmental systems (e.g., NASA's Earth Observation System). Remote-sensing systems require calibration with *in situ* measurements (e.g., "ground truth" measurements) and the historical experiences of intelligence systems may be of mutual benefit to the intelligence community, environmental researchers, and natural resource managers.

Another potential benefit of using intelligence data and systems is that the nonrecurring costs have already been paid for, and recurring costs to researchers can be low. The intelligence community can thus support the environmental missions of civil agencies such as the Department of the Interior and NOAA and contribute to interagency working groups such as the CENR without requiring these agencies to develop large, new programs at a time when discretionary spending is under great restraint. Intelligence data might be used by natural resource managers, such as the Bureau of Land Management, U.S. Forest Service, U.S. Park Service, and the Fish and Wildlife Service, who need to monitor large remote areas with limited resources. The benefits are not just domestic ones, but can be international as well since virtually all civil agencies engage in some form of international environmental cooperation. Intelligence data, especially when declassified, can constitute a significant U.S. contribution without requiring significant new spending.

On the cost side, the most obvious drawback of working with the IC is security. Protecting intelligence data requires complex and expensive physical and organizational measures.[1] It is expensive to review materials for declassification and open release. Agencies and private companies account for the cost of security in a wide variety of ways, so obtaining accurate estimates is difficult.[2] A less appreciated factor is the cost impact of security on productivity. Limitations on sharing information, reduced labor mobility, and transaction costs in getting and storing intelligence data increase the cost of working with such data above that of direct security charges.[3]

The productivity costs of using classified intelligence data can be prohibitive for applications such as international scientific research. The most fundamental problem is that classified data are not open for peer review. Even if appropriately cleared scientists are available to review work done within the national security community, the standard is generally that data used for scientific advances be available to all. In addition to scientific principles, open data sharing has value in terms of helping ensure the integrity of data and data products and validating ground truth measurements. In practice, there are allowable exceptions, such as limiting the availability of datasets to allow priority claims by principal investigators, but reliance on data that others cannot verify is not generally acceptable. Use of classified data can result in additional costs to independently verify research results.

An example of the significance of peer review is the debate over sea-level estimates by the Exxon oil company in the 1970s. Using proprietary geologic data, scientists at Exxon published a chart of average sea level versus year, extending far into the past. Because outside scientists were unable to review the original data, the analysis was

---

[1] *Redefining Security: A Report of the Joint Security Commission,* a report to the Secretary of Defense and the Director, Central Intelligence, Washington, D.C., February 28, 1994. See especially Chapter 9: "Cost of Security—An Illusive Target."

[2] One estimate is that about 70 percent of total security costs come from labor, 20 percent from facility and equipment costs, and the remaining costs are carried in overhead and not identified as security costs *per se.* Interview with Glen Gates, Lockheed Martin, Denver, Colorado, April 25, 1996.

[3] Interview with Peter Sanderholm, Security Policy Board, Arlington, Virgina, April 23, 1996.

not fully accepted. Public data from ocean cores are starting to confirm the Exxon data, and the earth sciences community is debating how to use the Exxon analyses in that the mechanism behind the most ancient sea-level swings remains unknown.[4] This situation is analogous to what would occur if new scientific claims were to be based on classified or proprietary data from government sources.

Outside of the scientific community, the use of intelligence data for environmental management can have costs other than accessing and protecting it. The uniqueness of intelligence data and the need to protect the means by which they are acquired can make the data difficult to use in regulatory applications such as stemming pollution. That is, classified data used to study pollution as a scientific phenomenon may not be usable to prosecute the polluter. Aside from limitations on the involvement of intelligence agencies in law enforcement (a continuing issue in drug smuggling), there is the question of the admissibility of intelligence data as evidence if it is not subject to challenge by defense counsel. Intelligence data may provide a helpful "cue" to finding pollution violations, but additional costs may be incurred in finding evidence for enforcement.

In terms of risks to commercial interests, a major concern of remote-sensing firms is that the U.S. government will directly compete with them and will undermine commercial markets by low-cost pricing of releasable intelligence data and/or products derived from intelligence data. This assumes that there are or may be comparable commercial products so that the intelligence data are not unique. While historical intelligence archives are clearly unique, the emerging availability of high-resolution commercial images from space provides a potential alternative to intelligence images. The government may not be able to charge market prices to minimize competition as U.S. policy (e.g., see OMB Circular A-130) for government data is that data be made available at the cost of reproduction and dissemination—essentially the lowest possible marginal cost. If intelligence data are made available, it would seem that government policy for other types of data would apply.

---

[4]"Ancient Sea-level Swings Confirmed," Richard A. Kerr, *Science*, Vol. 272, No. 5265, May 24, 1996, pp. 1097–1098.

If intelligence data were available for commercial environmental uses, firms that used such data may become dependent on the data and thus be exposed to government policy instability in addition to normal business risks. If access to intelligence data or, as is more likely, access to products derived from intelligence data were interrupted, firms would face financial losses depending on their degree of exposure, the availability of alternative sources, and the nature of customer demand. For example, geographic information systems (GIS) for oil exploration using intelligence-derived imagery information may face relatively few risks as commercial aerial and space images become available, and an interruption of a few months or even years may not be noticed by customers. A GIS for agriculture, however, or even urban mapping needs repeated high-resolution images, and data interruption would be less tolerable.

Ensuring against political risk is difficult and expensive and thus a potential cost to the use of intelligence data in commercial environmental applications. On the other hand, firms rely every day on government data and services, such as weather reports. It is also unlikely that commercial firms would have access to current forms of intelligence, such as imagery, except in special circumstances such as natural disasters. Thus, there would be an incentive for commercial systems to complement available intelligence sources.

NATIONAL SECURITY INTERESTS

The work of the MEDEA scientific advisory committee has shown potential benefits to the national security community from pursuing environmental applications for intelligence data and systems. In addition to helping with sensor calibration and validation, environmental scientists can assist in developing software algorithms and bringing the latest scientific research to intelligence analyses. In almost all areas of technology, commercial industry has moved ahead of the government, and environmental applications can provide a bridge to bring new skills into the intelligence community.

Indirect benefits of cooperation include attracting outside talent to the national security community and promoting greater use of open information sources. Working on environmental problems that can be openly discussed creates opportunities for international cooperation and cooperative validation of environmental data results. More subtle, and thus less demonstrable, benefits to the national security community include the broadening and strengthening of political support for military and national intelligence systems in a post–cold war world. The continued availability of such systems, combined with environmental use of the data, can help deter or co-opt the emergence of potential foreign competitor systems. The problem from a national perspective is that it may be U.S. commercial remote-sensing firms that are deterred or co-opted.

A common concern voiced about the use of intelligence data for environmental purposes is that such activities will compete for limited resources—people with special skills, funds, and the services of the intelligence systems themselves. However, based on experiences with MEDEA and the Government Applications Task Force, environmental applications do not place significant demands on intelligence systems. Budget constraints arise from concerns about whether such activities should be funded rather than affordability *per se.*[5]

The military and intelligence segments of the national security community have differing views on applying intelligence data and resources to environmental problems. In general, the military feels that defense issues should be the primary, if not the sole, DoD priority. There is little interest in nonmilitary environmental issues, however beneficial from a national perspective. However, military interest in environmental issues has increased in recent years as a result of requirements to maintain or improve environmental standards at its bases and facilities, including those being closed.[6] To this extent, the military supports using intelligence data as an aid to meeting environment requirements.

---

[5]An important exception arises in declassifying intelligence data, a process that can be expensive and time-consuming. Large amounts of non-environmental intelligence information are candidates for release, and the intelligence community places a relatively low priority on routine declassification. (When the CORONA images were released, the National Archives was made responsible for declassification, not the intelligence community.) There are no clear guidelines on whether and how to support public access to declassified data or the priority to give declassifying environmentally significant datasets.

[6]See, for example, D. Rubenson, M. D. Millot, G. Farnsworth, and J. Aroesty, *More Than 25 Million Acres? DoD as a Federal, Natural, and Cultural Resource Manager,* RAND, MR-715-OSD, 1996.

Intelligence community analysts and managers have a wider range of views. Some are adamantly opposed to any non-intelligence work, environmental or otherwise, that might compromise intelligence sources and methods (e.g., reverse engineering, security leaks, hostile intelligence penetrations, etc.) quite aside from direct budget costs. Others feel that supporting environmental work, as long as it is not to the neglect of traditional intelligence missions, should be a routine part of intelligence work for expected benefits to the nation as well as the intelligence community

Other risks for the intelligence community arise from policy debates and the potential impact on political support in general and classified funding in particular. The lack of direct support in presidential policy statements and legislation for routine use of intelligence data for environmental purposes leaves such efforts open to political and partisan criticism. If the IC is perceived as participating in activities inconsistent with its stated missions, there is the potential for Congress to reduce or eliminate the special procurement freedoms and budgetary discretion used in intelligence programs. The IC could be damaged if intelligence data used for environmental purposes is misused, whether unintentional (e.g., inadvertent disclosure) or intentional (leaks or violations of legal restrictions on targeting of U.S. persons).[7]

CONGRESSIONAL VIEWS OF BENEFITS, COSTS, AND RISKS

There is no consensus in the Congress on the overall benefits, costs, and risks of using intelligence data in environmental applications. Aside from a small number of committee chairmen, members have not paid attention to this issue, so the views of committee staffs are most influential. The staff have diverse opinions, with their sense of benefits, costs, and risks depending heavily on which committees they serve, followed by partisan leanings.

Staff for the committees of civil agencies, such as the House Science Committee and the Senate Committee on Commerce, Transportation, and Science, are very sensitive to budget limitations and

---

[7]For example, see Part 2.3(h) of Executive Order 12333, *Governing Intelligence Activities* (excerpts), December 4, 1981.

trade-offs. Virtually all civil agencies face declining real budgets and are cutting ongoing operations, and have little incentive to support even modest levels of new spending to exploit intelligence data. The data may be desirable to civil agencies, but staffers discount the potential benefits as being in competition with activities whose benefits are known. There are costs to developing expertise in using intelligence data and integrating it into routine operations. Again, staffers tend to see these immediate costs outweighing the prospect of greater agency effectiveness or new knowledge.

There is wide recognition of the importance of environmental issues and problems; however, there are major debates over environmental research generally and the role of governments and markets in dealing with environmental issues. These debates have become more partisan in recent years. While seemingly remote from immediate scientific questions on the utility of intelligence data, the symbolism of using intelligence data quickly leads to entanglement in larger political questions. Supporting the use of intelligence data is seen as approving of government spending for environmental research, which may result in greater government regulation of economic activity. The appearance of using intelligence data for developing and enforcing environmental regulation is seen as especially objectionable by some. Given this debate, some in Congress view the benefits of environmental work by the government as low and the potential political and economic risks as high.

On the other hand, many argue that more environmental research is needed to prevent inappropriate environmental regulations. They claim that scientific improvements and better environmental monitoring will enable movement away from traditional "command and control" types of regulation to a more flexible regulatory system that will achieve environmental benefits at less cost to industry. At the same time, improved understanding of the environment would facilitate cost-benefit analyses and create "performance-based" regulations. Such regulations, it is hoped, would be applied in a more equitable way across the country if timely and accurate environmental monitoring data were available. Both commercial and government sources could provide such data, with data from the intelligence community being but one option.

A potential set of environmental applications that could attract broad congressional support is promoting public safety via disaster mitigation. Intelligence data has been used to characterize disaster damage within the United States and overseas, so precedents can be cited.[8] Warning of natural disasters and providing relief is an option with immediate political benefits, and costs for domestic relief are relatively easy to support, with foreign relief only slightly less so. Timeliness of data would be of paramount importance.

Cooperation with the private sector is another area that could find common ground for political support of environmental applications. Some staff are concerned that the government will compete with an increasingly capable commercial remote-sensing industry. The U.S. government is already supporting major environmental monitoring efforts (e.g., the Earth Observation System) in which the role of private sector data sources is still being debated. These staff would urge the intelligence community to show that it is minimizing the risks of government competition by providing only unique capabilities and data that can not or will not be provided commercially, and that it is seeking to use commercial data and services wherever possible. These points form an interesting area of common concern and agreement between the congressional national security committees and those for civil agencies.

Within the national security committees, such as the House Permanent Select Committee on Intelligence and the Senate Armed Services Committee, budget constraints and trade-offs drive many issues. The first concern in using intelligence data for environmental purposes is that it not create a requirement for additional funding and conflict with existing priorities. To date, the desired resources appear to be marginal compared with other intelligence community activities. The next concern is with policy. Although skeptical, staffers are often ready to grant the potential benefit of intelligence data in environmental uses and that the budgetary impact would be low. They question what are the appropriate roles for the intelligence community, or even DoD as a whole, in environmental issues. The use of national security resources for environmental missions,

---

[8]"CIA Discloses Disaster Monitoring with National Space Systems," Associated Press, October 20, 1995. "Russian Spy Satellites to Save United States from Earthquakes and Greenhouse Effect," Leonid Mlechin, *Izvestiya*, July 22, 1995, p. 3.

however worthy, sets a precedent for using these resources for other public purposes, thus risking their diminution for basic national security objectives.

Conversely, there is the debate over the role of environmental factors in achieving national security objectives. Some staff support the idea that environmental degradation is a significant cause of regional instability and conflict whereas others contend that environmental factors are secondary to traditional political and cultural forces as the root of military conflict.[9] The use of intelligence data in environmental applications can come under criticism, not so much on the data's own merits but for the potential to support new interpretations of the causes of conflict. Promoting such uses is thus seen by some staff as politically risky even if a particular application is worthwhile.

Assessing the benefits, costs, and risks of using intelligence data outside of the intelligence community quickly leads to debates over excessive secrecy and the need for more declassification of intelligence community activities and information in general. Again, the particular merits of using intelligence data for environmental applications become a secondary factor. The declassification of certain types of intelligence data is seen as potentially leading to pressure for other kinds of intelligence information. Revealing the existence of some types of data can risk not only the "sources and methods" by which they were collected, but raise questions about why the data were collected in the first place, which can be more politically sensitive than the data themselves. The ambiguity surrounding the use of intelligence data for environmental purposes highlights the lack of a broader analytic framework for assessing intelligence products.

KEY FACTORS TO CONSIDER

The intelligence community has technical contributions it might make, but demand, cost, and acceptance questions remain. Deciding on the appropriate use of intelligence data and resources

---

[9]Debates over historical causes of conflict also occur among archaeologists interpreting early civilizations. See "California Social Climbers: Low Water Prompts High Status," Joshua Fischman, *Science*, May 10, 1996, pp. 811–812.

for environmental applications requires a balancing of potential benefits, costs, and risks across multiple interest groups. Any specific application has ramifications for scientific value, budgetary impact, and political risk; nonetheless, a few key factors appear time and again as general considerations.

First, what is the demand from potential users? However many demonstrations and experiments occur, it is civil agencies, scientists, and commercial firms that will decide whether the routine use of intelligence data for environmental purposes is worthwhile. There must be a demand for the data, as market acceptance can not be forced. Although some data may be unique, there may be little demand for it outside of the intelligence community. There may be commercial and civil alternatives to some types of data (e.g., IMINT) and thus demand will depend on factors such as accuracy, timeliness, and ease of use.

The second factor is the cost of using intelligence data, which has multiple aspects. There is the direct cost to the user of accessing intelligence data. There are security costs, both direct and indirect, from handling classified data. For the intelligence community, there is the direct cost of working with outside users and the potential risk of compromising security. The cost of declassification and archive maintenance may be paid by either the supplier or the consumer of data. These costs tend to be immediate, whereas savings in security infrastructure arising from reduced classification will occur in the future.

The third factor is the acceptability of intelligence data to various environmental communities. Even if the cost and benefit of using intelligence data are attractive, doing so can be impractical if it cannot be peer-reviewed by uncleared scientists, accepted in court, or trusted by commercial customers. Acceptability is more than a question of prejudice, but a potential legal consideration as well. How intelligence data will be priced, what uses are allowed, who is granted access, and how privacy rights are respected can be just as important as immediate technical benefits.

Finally, there are political and policy risks that may arise in Congress. As discussed earlier, these risks are often less about the use of intelligence data in environmental applications *per se* and more about the political implications of such use. A noteworthy practical considera-tion is how and where environmental applications of intelligence data are funded—within intelligence community budgets, the DoD budget, or civil agency budgets. Aside from affordability considera-tions, where an activity is placed determines which statutory au-thority applies and which congressional committees have jurisdic-tion.

The intelligence community enjoys great flexibility in the manage-ment of its activities compared with most federal agencies, which makes it an attractive place for experimental activities. This flexibil-ity also carries constraints, however, in that the results of its pro-grams tend to be classified, thus limiting their utility to open pro-grams such as environmental research. A major unresolved question is whether it is possible to combine the relative freedom found within classified programs with the routine work of civil agencies. It may turn out that environmental applications of intelligence data can be sustained only at relatively low funding levels consistent with the ability of civil agencies to pay, rather than at higher levels that might be justified by technical considerations alone.

Chapter Four

ALTERNATIVE APPROACHES TO PROVIDING INTELLIGENCE DATA FOR ENVIRONMENTAL USES

At present, there is no agreed upon mechanism or institutional home within either a civil agency or the intelligence community through which intelligence data may be used for environmental purposes (even assuming there was agreement on what to do). Corresponding to the various viewpoints on using intelligence data for environmental purposes, several alternative mechanisms could be implemented. This chapter describes these alternatives and their major characteristics. All of the alternatives assume that there is no policy prohibition on using intelligence data for environmental purposes outside of the intelligence community, although there may be varying constraints.

INSTITUTIONAL MECHANISMS

Institutional mechanisms to facilitate the use of intelligence data for environmental applications will have to address data access itself and the support systems for data management and interpretation. Defining the terms and conditions of data access requires criteria on who and how individuals gain access. For example, security clearances are required for access to classified data and additional direct or indirect fees may be imposed to recover the resulting costs.[1] Although clearances are not required for access to unclassified data, access may be limited to U.S. citizens or international organizations

---

[1] For example, direct fees may be applied to a specific user for access to specific data while an indirect fee is charged to a user organization for more generalized access by organization members.

with specific data-sharing agreements. Again, direct or indirect fees can be charged. Also, a particular institutional mechanism may or may not be responsible for declassifying data received from other parts of the intelligence community.

Support systems for using intelligence data go beyond merely providing access. At a minimum, support can include the use of U.S. government facilities and services through which intelligence data are handled. Support may be more elaborate, as with government R&D and industry partnerships to develop new technologies and applications for exploiting intelligence data. As part of the terms and conditions of access, support systems may place restrictions on data use such as barring commercial uses or export (assuming it is not already in the public domain). Such restrictions may be implemented by simple notification of users or complex encryption systems.

Three major factors determine how intelligence data for environmental applications might be accessed (see Table 2). The first, user security, is whether the users go to the data or the data go to the user. The second, interface style, is whether data from different intelligence sources are accessed through separate processes or through a common process at a common center. The third, data status, is whether the data are discontinued, old, or otherwise less sensitive or current and still sensitive. Combinations of these factors suggest varying levels of control over data and users seeking access. For example, discontinued and old data may still be classified but be made available at a common archive rather than at separate secure facilities. This would provide for easier user access while maintaining an

Table 2

Major Access Factors

Access Factor	High Control	Low Control
User security	Users go inside a central secure facility	Data released from one or more facilities to multiple users
Interface style	Data sources accessed separately	All data sources accessed at a common point
Data status	Current and sensitive data	Discontinued and old data

appropriate level of security. Other combinations of access factors would not make sense, however, such as allowing current intelligence data to go to a nonsecure facility.

From combinations of the three access factors, five general institutional mechanisms suggest themselves. These mechanisms proceed from high-control to low-control forms with security measures being the most significant discriminator:

- Program-by-program access within the intelligence community

- A single access center within the U.S. government

- A secure U.S. government archive facility only for discontinued/old but still classified data

- An open access center within the U.S. government for unclassified data

- Decentralized access to unclassified data inside or out of the U.S. government (e.g., using the Internet).

INSTITUTIONAL ALTERNATIVES

There are several institutions that might house the mechanisms listed above. The various combinations of a particular mechanism with an institutional home give us the major alternatives for decisionmakers who would like to make intelligence data available for environmental uses. Each of the major alternatives is discussed below.

Intelligence Community Center

An environmental center could be created within the intelligence community to serve as a focal point for outside users. This center would operate in a manner similar to other intelligence centers, such as those for narcotics, terrorism, and counterproliferation. The center would provide access to and support in using intelligence data, potentially including current as well as older datasets. Access to the secure facility would be limited to cleared personnel, although unclassified derived products could leave the center for wider distribution.

Funding would come from contributions by civil and military agencies using the center, as well as the intelligence community itself. Private sector users, such as universities and corporations, might have access but would be expected to pay a user fee. The goal would be for the center to have a minimal impact on the intelligence community's, budget, consistent with tangible and intangible benefits received.

A key aspect of the center would be the "one-stop shop" that would eliminate the need for program-by-program access decisions. The need to reduce or eliminate intelligence "stovepipes" has been promoted by the military services and acknowledged by the intelligence agencies. Such centralization, while convenient, carries a security risk as compartmentation of programs is reduced. This may be an acceptable risk if the center limits itself to data and derived products without providing significant insight into the systems that provide the data. Whether this would be acceptable to the data users would remain to be seen.

An intelligence community center could provide continuing opportunities for interactions between environmental researchers and intelligence analysts, analogous to the work of MEDEA and the Environmental Working Group. Experience with intelligence centers has shown there are drawbacks, however. Often there is a perception that the centers really belong to the Central Intelligence Agency, rather than to the intelligence community as a whole. There are likely to be problems with ensuring stable funding if contributions from more than one agency are required. The staffing of the centers can be a challenge if highly skilled persons are reluctant to take a chance on an institution whose activities are seen as secondary to the mission of their home agencies or as having an uncertain future.

Department of Defense Center

An alternative home for an environmental center is the Department of Defense. Again, it would be a central, secure facility to which environmental researchers and civil agencies could come for access to intelligence data. A potential model for a defense-oriented center is the U.S. Navy Meteorology & Oceanography Command (NAVOCEAN), based in Stennis, Mississippi. This facility combines data from a variety of intelligence sources to support U.S. naval operations worldwide. It works with the Naval Research Laboratory on leading-edge oceanographic research and has access to the world's leading ocean scientists. The combination of multiple information sources, leading scientists, and sophisticated modeling and computer simulation capabilities could be a model for civil environmental activities such as NASA's Mission-to-Planet Earth.

An important management or cultural characteristic of NAVOCEAN is that it sees its mission as "serving the Fleet" as opposed to conducting environmental research *per se*. This seems to provide an important focus for NAVOCEAN's work, promote acceptance by the rest of the U.S. Navy, and create an incentive to support scientific research. A DoD center that supported civil environmental applications would be unlikely to have a focused combat support mission, yet the DoD as a whole has environmental problems that could benefit from interactions with civil communities. The NAVOCEAN experience can provide useful examples and precedents for handling such interactions.[2]

Funding would come from contributions by civil agencies using the center, as well as the Department of Defense. Private sector users might find working with DoD less daunting than with the intelligence community, but they would likely still have to pay some sort of user fee. A possible home for a DoD center may be the National Imagery and Mapping Agency (NIMA). This would concentrate skills in the type of intelligence data most likely to be in demand (i.e., imagery), with the option of adding other skills as needed. NIMA is intended to support all military services, so additional interactions with civil agencies should not pose a major additional burden.[3] On the other hand, an emphasis on DoD issues could limit the use of resources for national or global issues that civil researchers and agencies may be interested in.

---

[2]The U.S. Navy's long historical relationship with the U.S. oceanographic community aids military-scientific cooperation. Efforts to build cooperation between the intelligence and environmental communities will not have this starting advantage.

[3]"Imagery, Mapping Agency's Client Focus Drives Agility," Clarence A. Robinson, Jr., *Signal*, April 1996, pp. 39–42.

Civil Agency Center

Civil agencies are thought to be the likely beneficiaries of greater access to intelligence data, so another option is to locate an environmental center within a civil agency. Candidate agencies might be the Department of the Interior, specifically the U.S. Geological Survey or the Department of Commerce's NOAA. These agencies handle classified data and have routine working relations with the intelligence community. A center established in a civil agency would represent a commitment to the routine use of intelligence data and the likely creation of new or expanded facilities.

A civil agency center would likely find easier acceptance by the various environmental communities, including civilian environmental scientists, natural resource managers, and state and local government decisionmakers. Nonfederal users would have a convenient point of access. On the other hand, the creation of an acceptable secure facility is likely to challenge civil agency budgets and cultures, and the intelligence community may be reluctant to share information from current intelligence systems. Thus, a civil center may end up with historical material that has been declassified or downgraded from higher classification levels.

A civil center would be difficult to sustain by one agency alone, and multiagency contributions would be necessary, more so than with a DoD or intelligence community center. In addition, the more open nature of the civil agency budget would result in closer public and congressional scrutiny and thus greater pressure to link center activities closely to agency missions. On the other hand, environmental activities do directly support the missions of civil agencies such as NOAA and the USGS. Their smaller budgets, however, compared with those in the national security community, would likely require budget justification along narrow mission lines.

Privatized Center

An alternative to having a U.S. government center would be to establish one in the private sector, perhaps at a university or contractor facility. As with a government center, access could be provided to intelligence data for approved persons and purposes. It is unlikely that a private center would have access to current intelligence systems and data. Consequently, such a center would more likely be an archive for old, but still classified, data as well as unclassified data. Such a center could reach out to remote users through the Internet and cooperate with private remote-sensing and GIS firms. It should be readily accepted by environmental communities, such as scientists, public and private natural resource managers, and policymakers.

A private center may require continuing government support yet would represent less of a commitment than a government center for environmental use of intelligence data. Unlike a government facility, a private center would have greater incentive to recover its costs and tailor its services and products to customer demand. Commercial firms are, however, likely to be concerned about government competition. A private center might face restrictions on the kinds of commercial practices it could engage in as well as security limitations.

Access fees for government data are likely to be critical to the financial viability of a private center. Assuming the data are still owned by the U.S. government, data policy rules would seem to limit fees to no more than the cost of reproduction and dissemination (marginal access costs). Fees might be charged for derived products and value-added services (such as searches) in accessing data archives. It is unlikely that such fees would be enough to sustain a center independent of reliable government funding. In short, U.S. government agencies supporting a private center would subsidize access to intelligence data for nongovernment users.

Maximum Declassification (No Centers)

Another alternative would be to abandon the idea of a special environmental center for intelligence data and promote declassification instead. The automatic declassification date for old data could be moved up from 25 years to, say, 10 years. Instead of funding a center, civil and military agencies could fund declassification reviews and the placement of data in the public domain as rapidly as possible. Access could be provided through a government agency, just as the USGS EROS facility provides access to declassified CORONA images.

Maximizing declassification would allow use of the data for all types of activities, not just environmental ones. The data would be open to peer review, thus removing one of the key objections to using intelligence data in the scientific community. Declassification would reduce the immediate costs of handling the data. A related issue is the uncertainty in determining any cost to national security of declassification and what compensatory measures might be needed.

The key challenge to implementing this alternative is the declassification review process and whether the intelligence community would be supportive. Movement toward greater declassification of intelligence data has found increasing support in Congress, but there are many competing priorities for attention. Environmental applications might be able to get higher priority if civil agencies are willing to fund the declassification of datasets of greatest interest to their missions. Scientific reviews by groups such as MEDEA can identify promising data for declassification. In particular, they can advise on how much, if any, information about the intelligence system that acquired the data needs to be declassified to judge the integrity and utility of the data.

Networks Versus Centers

One might question the desirability of a special center for environmental uses of intelligence data while still recognizing the utility of classified sources. Users have different access needs—some may be content with unclassified products derived from intelligence data, others may want to see the original data, and some will want access to the intelligence collection systems themselves. Instead of a single center, there might be a network of centers with varying missions, user communities, and levels of security. The network could be connected by secure telephone, fax, and videoconferencing, and thus be able to form "virtual centers" for particular applications.

Imagine a series of concentric rings with intelligence collection and data management systems at the center, perhaps the NRO and NIMA. The systems would be compartmented on a program-by-program basis within the intelligence community. The first inner ring is composed of organizations needing access to intelligence data but not operational control of the collection systems. Examples include MEDEA, NAVOCEAN, and the USGS Advanced Systems Center.

The second ring has domestic organizations that use derived products but that may need access to intelligence data from time to time. Examples here are the NOAA Hurricane Center and the Pacific Disaster Center in Hawaii. Finally, the third and outer ring has international organizations that exchange data or collaborate on common missions and thus deal almost exclusively with unclassified data and derived products. Examples include the Gore-Chernomyrdin Commission's Environmental Working Group and the U.S.-Japan Earthquake Center.

The emerging network approach is a likely "default" result if no new policy initiatives are made. It has the advantage of allocating funding responsibilities to the agencies interested in using intelligence data. It does not require major changes to U.S. security procedures, although greater declassification and reduced security compartments would occur. The disadvantage is that intelligence data may be underutilized compared with a single access center devoted to environmental applications. Another disadvantage is that greater overhead costs are likely to be incurred as a result of redundant organizations within the various user agencies, much like the criticism that led to the NIMA proposal.

EVALUATION CRITERIA

There are two general categories of evaluation criteria for alternative organizational structures. There are those that deal with the organizations' effectiveness in performing the stated mission, and those that deal with the political feasibility of implementing and sustaining such an organization. The two sets of criteria are different in that one judges how well an organization might perform and the other judges whether the organization will be formed at all. In a completely objective decisionmaking process, these metrics might be identical. In practice they are different because of the different viewpoints of the groups that share the power of decision.

Measures of Effectiveness

Institutional measures of effectiveness (MOE) typically evaluate the accomplishment of a stated mission, the efficient use of resources, and compliance with any special constraints. Useful metrics represent measurable quantities that are controllable by the institution performing a specific mission. MOE categories for the use of intelligence data in environmental applications might be

- contribution to agency missions

- operational outputs

- productivity

- security.

The first criterion, contribution to agency missions, is important from an agency point of view but may not be significant from a national perspective. In the absence of a broader measure of social welfare, however, agency relevance is a useful proxy when combined with specific outcome judgments: how important are environmental issues to the agency and how important are intelligence data and resources to environmental issues. These multiple judgments determine priorities for ongoing operations and future plans. This assumes the agency itself contributes to the national interest or it would not be funded.

Environmental research and analyses help support the missions of many government agencies today. Different institutional homes will naturally, however, have different mission objectives. For example, a special-access center established within the Department of Defense will be evaluated on how well it supports military operations, as opposed to a civil agency center that supports management of natural resources.

Operational outputs independent of the institutional location can include metrics such as the number of participating organizations and requests supported, and the range and quality of datasets, derived products, and support services made available. Commercial, military, and university organizations can provide benchmarks for the provision of other types of information-based services. These metrics deal with how much is done rather than whether it is useful or productive.

Closely related to operational benchmarks are MOEs that deal with the productivity of suppliers and users. Supplier productivity measures address how efficiently budget resources are used—the number of staff required to support user requests, the time to process requests, and prices charged. Since the intelligence community is not (and should not) be in the business of making a financial profit, there can be MOEs to measure the "flow back" of other benefits. These benefits might be the improvement of internal skills and processes that support intelligence missions and more efficient utilization of specialized facilities and equipment. User productivity measures are a primary reason for making intelligence data available in the first place. For scientific researchers, productivity can be the quality of peer-reviewed publications. For civil agencies, it can mean cost efficiencies in managing natural resources, producing geographic information systems, or monitoring the environment.

Efficiency metrics include the ability to generate output at low cost, within constraints such as security. The use of intelligence data carries special security responsibilities and constraints. Classification, compartmentation, physical and managerial access limits, the "need-to know" principle, and counterintelligence measures are all used to ensure that only approved persons obtain intelligence data. Determining the best security MOEs is an intensely debated subject in its own right that is beyond the scope of this report. Nonetheless, MOEs that reduce the number of persons with access are usually in tension with other mission objectives such as widespread dissemination of scientific results.

Rather than bringing users to the data, data can be declassified and brought to users via central archives or the Internet. Declassification processes have their own MOEs, such as time, cost, volume, and treatment of priority requests. In addition to original data, declassification MOEs can apply to derived products where the data source and method are protected but decisions about releasability are needed. After declassification, the government can place a restriction on data dissemination and use that protects its intellectual property interests as distinct from national security. Depending on policy objectives, the government can take a variety of actions, such as putting data in the public domain, limiting access to U.S. citizens, and prohibiting commercial uses.

Selection Criteria

Selection criteria can cover outcomes (e.g., contribution to national interests), outputs (e.g., specific products), efficiency, and feasibility (both technical and political). Selection criteria for choosing how to make intelligence data available for environmental uses can be thought of as emerging from the constellation of relevant stakeholders and national interests. Based on interviews and literature reviews, we see the following criteria as being the most crucial:

- Affordability

- Technical merit

- Security risks

- Institutional constraints and preferences

- External acceptance.

This set of criteria emphasizes feasibility issues, which were of concern to potential stakeholders. Prior work by the ETF and MEDEA appear to have answered the question of technical desirability. Ultimately, decisionmakers will apply weights to represent the relative value of these criteria in recommending a preferred option. MOEs then become a concern for implementation and management.

The first, and possibly most decisive criterion, is affordability—total cost, the willingness of agencies to pay, and funding stability. It may be easier to pick an expensive option in a large agency than a cheaper option in an agency with fewer resources. Another consideration is that some options involve completely new costs whereas others involve marginal increases to existing costs. A prime example is the cost of security for a civil as opposed to an intelligence agency. While contributions from all who benefit may be desirable and equitable, single agency funding can be more stable than relying on multiple agencies that can seek to shift their burden to others during each legislative cycle.

The technical merit of each alternative approach is a necessary consideration. By technical merit, we mean the value of conducting specific environmental studies as well as the utility of using intelligence data in a specific study. For scientific studies, value is traditionally established by competitive peer review. Evaluations of technical merit can include awareness of past experiences and demonstrations—state-of-the-art knowledge of environmental research and information technologies, and relevant relationships with commercial and scientific communities. Additional considerations are implementation times and costs for a specific approach. Some centers may be created quickly whereas networks of centers may take years to emerge and integrate.

Perceived and actual security risks are a consideration whenever intelligence data are involved. As noted earlier, there are intrinsic tensions between security and non-intelligence environmental uses. Depending on broader policy decisions for classified data handling and declassification, the use of intelligence data for environmental purposes could become routine or remain an experimental curiosity. The cultural mismatch between the environmental and intelligence communities can influence the selection of more extreme options— access to very few people or open access to very small amounts of data. A particular institutional approach will have to balance the need for compliance with security rules with user demands for convenience, low costs, and wide acceptance of intelligence-derived products.[4]

After affordability, the most important selection criteria are potential institutional constraints and preferences, a complex mix of legal, policy, and cultural factors that can determine whether using intelligence data for environmental purposes is ever "accepted" within the government bureaucracy. A center located in the intelligence community comes under the authority of the National Security Act of 1947 and Title 50, Chapter 15 of the Code of Federal Regulation. One located in the Defense Department comes under Title 10. Where a particular government activity is placed in the federal budget and the cognizant legal authority are vital political considerations for congressional support and oversight assignments.

---

[4]Certain advanced computers, software, and remote-sensing technologies are controlled by U.S. export regulations. These regulations should not be an issue, however, as the international transfer of controlled technology and equipment is not a requirement for environmental uses. Unclassified environmental information *per se* is not controlled.

Institutional placement carries explicit and implied policy preferences in the priority given to military, civil, commercial, or national
intelligence objectives. An environmental center placed within a
single service (e.g., the U.S. Navy) may be able to serve broader national objectives although the center will not be its primary mission.
Similarly, an environmental center supported by civil agency and
commercial fees will likely give priority to near-term environmental
applications as opposed to open-ended scientific research. These
policy preferences should be consistent with the culture of the cho-
sen host institution. It would be a clear mistake to place a secure intelligence center within NASA's Mission to Planet Earth program, for
example, given both NASA's open culture and the need to work with
scientists from many countries.

The final selection criterion is related to the issue of acceptance, but
concerns communities external to the U.S. government. The potential use of intelligence data is both a cachet and a burden. Varying
reactions will be found in the international, scientific, and commercial communities that the U.S. government deals with. In addition to
the concerns of the scientific community with peer review and the
commercial community with government competition, there are
foreign policy concerns. Some countries with a long history of intelligence cooperation with the United States (e.g., the United
Kingdom, Canada, and Australia) would find the extension of such
cooperation into more open environmental work a natural one.
Former adversaries, such as Russia, would see such cooperation as
part of a broader pattern of building better relationships. Countries
such as Japan may have domestic constraints on overt cooperation
on military and intelligence matters, even something as seemingly
benign as environmental monitoring.[5] An environmental center
placed within the intelligence community would have a different acceptance problem than one placed in a civil agency or the private
sector.

Finally, and most important, there is the issue of acceptance by the
American people. While there is broad support for efforts supporting

---

[5]Japan's post-war constitution has in the past been interpreted by the Diet as barring
the development of military reconnaissance satellites and limiting the use of foreign
systems. The Japan Defense Agency has, however, been allowed to acquire
commercial remote-sensing images. This situation may change in the near future.

a healthier and safer environment and making the most efficient use of federal resources, the use of intelligence data carries a special burden. Like their representatives in Congress, the public can have mixed feelings about the capabilities and functioning of the intelligence community. Watchdogs would oppose resources being spent on what might appear to be "frivolous" activities and they would be wary of any potential abuse of intelligence sources and methods that could compromise U.S. security or civil liberties. The latter point is sometimes difficult to get across to persons in the national security community, who are keenly aware of the legal constraints placed on their activities. Yet it is important that efforts to improve environmental monitoring not give even the appearance of "domestic spying" or the taking on of law enforcement functions. If it does, political support even for experimental application of intelligence data will quickly vanish.

EXAMPLE RANKING OF ALTERNATIVES

The six institutional alternatives can be ranked in order of preference using the five selection criteria. A notional example is shown in Table 3. Alternatives were ranked from 1 (best) to 6 (worst) in order

Table 3

Ranking of Institutional Alternatives

Alternatives	Criteria				
	Affordability	Technical Merit	Security Risk	Institutional	External Acceptance
Intelligence center = 3.8	5	3	2	4	5
Defense department center = 4.2	4	5	3	5	4
Civil agency center = 3.6	6	2	4	3	3
Privatized center = 5.0	3	4	6	6	6
Maximum declassification only = 2.0	1	6	1	1	1
Networks versus centers = 2.4	2	1	5	2	2

of how well they met each selection criterion. Given equal weighting of criteria, the alternative with the lowest average score is best. In general, the selection criteria are such that alternatives that minimize potential problems do better, which means lowering security risks and the likelihood of rejection as opposed to maximizing technical output. As noted earlier, the need to balance multiple interests and viewpoints will necessarily result in a somewhat subjective answer.

If all criteria are treated as equally important, the alternative of declassifying as much data as possible is preferred. This is followed by the creation of a network of centers rather than a single special-access center. These choices did well because they were more affordable and required minimal risks in terms of cultural acceptance inside or outside of the government. The declassification option did not result in the kinds of technical interactions that could benefit the intelligence community or environmental researchers. The network option has security risks with the wide variety of organizations having access to sensitive information or products.

Next in order of preference is the creation of a special-access center within a civil agency or the intelligence community. The civil agency option provides the most opportunities for technical interchange and collaborative work, but may not be affordable given recent budgets. The intelligence agency option also does well in terms of technical merit and very well in terms of security, but it too has affordability problems. An intelligence center will also have more external acceptance problems than a civil agency, especially for international users.

At the bottom are a DoD or private center, which are problematic for many reasons, but especially in terms of what mission is to be served. A DoD center would have combat support as its top priority, as it should, and a private center would require government subsidies and access to sensitive data yet remain outside of direct government control.

OBSERVATIONS AND RECOMMENDATIONS

SUMMARY OBSERVATIONS

The U.S. intelligence community is undergoing debates about its future roles, organization, and capabilities. This reflects a fundamental change from serving one customer, the President, to serving many customers in different agencies and communities. The environmental community of researchers and managers is a potential consumer of intelligence data and resources. Determining the most appropriate and effective relationship between the intelligence community and the environmental community is a complex task with many competing viewpoints. Given this task, there is a strong need for a strategic framework in which to assess intelligence community roles and for a mechanism with which to deal with issues, such as environmental monitoring, that cross traditional federal agency boundaries.

Experiments and demonstrations to date, almost all of which are classified in one form or another, have shown that intelligence data and capabilities can make significant contributions to civilian and national security-related environmental issues. The contributions span a spectrum from using unique datasets that advance basic scientific knowledge to the use of specialized skills that can enhance the ability of civil agencies in their environmental missions. The flow of benefits is not one-way—there are direct and indirect benefits to the intelligence community from greater interactions with outside scientists and agencies. These benefits include improving and stretching the skills of the intelligence community and making greater use of data from open sources.

The NAVOCEAN facility in Stennis, Mississippi provides an attractive model of how intelligence data might be used for civil environmental applications. It routinely combines data from all types of sources (e.g., space, ground, and ocean-based, classified and open) with advanced modeling and simulation capabilities to support the U.S. Navy's operational missions. There are strong science-driven interactions with relevant civil communities (e.g., oceanographers) and additional in-house expertise is available through the Naval Research Laboratory.

Civil environmental applications of intelligence data have generally been opportunistic rather than routine, with a few notable exceptions (e.g., the U.S. Geological Survey). Only small numbers of civil environmental researchers and managers have had access to intelligence datasets because of the limitations imposed by classification. A transition to a more stable and routine relationship between the intelligence and environmental communities is possible and should be beneficial to the nation, but the constraints on that transition are many.

The most difficult issue is the policy uncertainty stemming from unresolved debates over intelligence community involvement in civil environmental issues, as well as more general debates over intelligence and environmental policy. The next most difficult issue is the lack of civil agency resources (e.g., funds, skilled personnel, facilities, etc.) to support exploration and exploitation of intelligence data for environmental purposes. A new and increasingly important factor in these policy debates in the growing strength of the commercial information industry generally and emergence of a commercial remote-sensing industry. Private industry can benefit from as well as be hurt by environmental applications of intelligence data.

The task for decisionmakers is to balance the many competing interests of civil, military, scientific, commercial, and intelligence stakeholders. A narrow interpretation of national security interests would support continued compartmentation and classification of all intelligence data with access (if any) only through a central, special-access facility. On the other hand, traditional scientific and civil agency interests would support maximum declassification of and decentralized access to environmental data from any source. Commercial interests would be best served by decentralized open access to declassified data, but only from obsolete intelligence sources such that the data are of a fixed, or at least predictable, amount. Finally, both commercial and national security interests would likely be harmed by open access to data from current intelligence sources. The government data and derived products would likely compete with and deter commercial competition while placing intelligence sources and methods at risk.

The President and Congress are both crucial to creating a stable policy framework for environmental uses of intelligence data. The President is still the most important "customer" for the intelligence community and sets policy and priorities through a variety of instruments. Within the current Administration, the National Science and Technology Council and the National Security Council appear to have overlapping responsibilities for the environmental use of intelligence data. It would be helpful in reducing policy uncertainty if there were a single point of responsibility or a joint mechanism for addressing the cross-cutting issues described in this report.

Congress is not only a source of funds, but the forum in which legislative compromises between competing interest groups are made, independent of the Executive Branch. The intelligence community needs presidential direction, but it also needs legislation that has bipartisan support for environmental efforts to outlast any one Administration.

OPEN QUESTIONS

This study has not addressed several other important, open questions. These deal with specific costs and risks that are best treated in less-open discussions. For example:

- Can all discontinued and old environmental data (>10 years) be declassified?
  — What would it cost?
  — Should it be done?

- What are the net risks and benefits of greater interactions between military/intelligence users and commercial/scientific users?

    — Is the answer significantly different for classified as opposed to declassified data and derived products?

- For which civil/commercial environmental purposes are intelligence data a unique technical resource?

    — Under what terms and conditions do intelligence data compete with or deter other data sources?

RECOMMENDATIONS

Our recommendations fall into two general categories: actions the intelligence community and the U.S. government should take and actions that it should not. Within these categories, there is a difference between the treatment of datasets that already exist and those that might be acquired by intelligence sources and methods.

- With the many private sector sensitivities surrounding the use of intelligence data for environmental purposes, specific policy guidance should be provided on what the government will *not* do, as well as what it might. Such guidance might say, for example, that the government will not

    — compete with or deter private sector activities,

    — declassify remote-sensing data that it would not license a commercial operator to collect (e.g., high-resolution imagery), and

    — provide access to original data from currently operational, classified systems for any commercial purpose.

- The Administration should promote cooperation on environmental research and management at multiple levels—interagency, international, the private sector, and state and local governments. Cooperative activities should promote the formation of networks on specific environmental concerns, such as natural disaster monitoring, that provide a mission for intelligence data applications.

- The intelligence community should become a regular participant in interagency environmental fora such as the NSTC's Committee on Environment and Natural Resources. Such participation would provide further opportunities to identify areas of cooperation in environmental research and management and promote wider awareness of the potential benefits of using intelligence data.

- While a lead role for the Department of Interior is a useful expedient, the Administration should seek a greater diversity of funding for civil environmental applications of intelligence data. Modest funding contributions could be of significant help to declassifying selected environmental datasets.

- With the formation of the National Imagery and Mapping Agency, the use of intelligence data for civil environmental applications should be included as a potential joint mission for the DoD and the intelligence community. This mission should be secondary, however, to the performance of traditional security functions.

- Greater effort should be devoted to declassifying environmental datasets held by the intelligence community and the Department of Defense. Particular attention should be given to data more than 10 years old and from intelligence systems that are no longer operational.

- The intelligence community should institute dialog with industry interests that may be affected by greater access to intelligence data for environmental uses. Dialog should include commercial firms with and without past experience on classified contracts, and firms engaged in gathering as well as processing remotely sensed data. The primary purpose would be to promote cooperation and trust by providing early private sector input on government policies and operations.

Presidential direction and bipartisan congressional support are necessary for the sustained use of intelligence data for environmental purposes. Some applications are more controversial than others and any effort to secure authorizing legislation should focus on applications with the widest possible basis of support. A likely first candidate might be natural disaster monitoring, which has a clear public safety mission, past precedents in the use of intelligence data, and potential benefit for state and local communities. Such communities typically lack the resources to support a major monitoring infrastructure that is already in place and available to the federal government.

Because disaster monitoring may overlap with commercial capabilities, early dialog with industry would be helpful in finding areas of cooperation (e.g., purchase of commercial data), controlling costs, and focusing intelligence contributions on unique niches. The securing of an external support base can be a long and difficult process, but the process of workshops, hearings, and the crafting of legislation is necessary to find common ground between the intelligence and environmental communities.

U.S. GOVERNMENT STATEMENTS

There are few published U.S. government policy statements on the use of intelligence data for environmental purposes. This appendix includes three such statements: relevant excerpts from the current National Space Policy, an Executive Order on the release of imagery from space-based national intelligence reconnaissance systems, and a speech by the Director of Central Intelligence (DCI).

The National Space Policy, released September 19, 1996, makes unclassified the fact that satellite photoreconnaissance systems can be used to collect data on natural or man-made disasters, and that such data can be disseminated to authorized federal agencies. This policy statement was developed through the National Science and Technology Council and is implemented as a Presidential Decision Directive. Excerpts from the section on "National Security Space Guidelines" include:

(7) Intelligence Space Sector Guidelines:

(a) The DCI shall ensure that the intelligence space sector provides timely information and data to support foreign, defense and economic policies; military operations; diplomatic activities; indications and warning; crisis management; and treaty verification, and that the sector performs research and development related to these functions.

(b) The DCI shall continue to develop and apply advanced technologies that respond to changes in the threat environment and support national intelligence priorities.

(c) The DCI shall work closely with the Secretary of Defense to improve the intelligence space sector's ability to support military operations worldwide.

(d) The nature, the attributable collected information and the operational details of intelligence space activities will be classified. The DCI shall establish and implement policies to provide appropriate protection for such data, including provisions for the declassification and release of such information when the DCI deems that protection is no longer required.

(e) Collected information that cannot be attributed to space systems will be classified according to its content.

(f) These guidelines do not apply to imagery product, the protection of which is governed by Executive Order 12951.

(g) Strict security procedures will be maintained to ensure that public discussion of satellite reconnaissance by Executive Branch personnel and contractors is consistent with DCI guidance. Executive Branch personnel and contractors should refrain from acknowledging or releasing information regarding satellite reconnaissance until a security review has been made.

(h) The following facts are UNCLASSIFIED:

(i) That the United States conducts satellite photoreconnaissance for peaceful purposes, including intelligence collection and monitoring arms control agreements.

(ii) That satellite photoreconnaissance includes a near real-time capability and is used to provide defense-related information for indications and warning, and the planning and conduct of military operations.

(iii) That satellite photoreconnaissance is used in the collection of mapping, charting, and geodetic data and such data is provided to authorized federal agencies.

(iv) That satellite photoreconnaissance is used to collect mapping, charting and geodetic data to develop global geodetic and cartographic materials to support defense and other mapping-related activities.

(v) That satellite photoreconnaissance can be used to collect scientific and environmental data and data on natural or man-made disasters, and such data can be disseminated to authorized federal agencies.

(vi) That photoreconnaissance assets can be used to image the United States and its territories and possessions.

(vii) That the U.S. conducts overhead signals intelligence collection.

(viii) That the U.S. conducts overhead measurement and signature intelligence collection.

(ix) The existence of the National Reconnaissance Office (NRO) and the identification and official titles of its senior officials. All other details, facts and products of intelligence space activities are subject to appropriate classification and security controls as determined by the DCI.

(i) Changes to the space intelligence security policy set forth in the national space policy can be authorized only by the President.

Executive Order 12951, released on February 24, 1995, deals with the public release of historical intelligence imagery from the CORONA, ARGON, and LANYARD missions of the 1960s. The Executive Order also directed the DCI to establish a program for the periodic review of other imagery systems for possible public release.

THE WHITE HOUSE

Office of the Press Secretary

For Immediate Release   February 24, 1995

EXECUTIVE ORDER
- - - - - - - -

RELEASE OF IMAGERY ACQUIRED BY SPACE-BASED
NATIONAL INTELLIGENCE RECONNAISSANCE SYSTEMS

By the authority vested in me as President by the Constitution and the laws of the United States of America and in order to release certain scientifically or environmentally useful imagery acquired by space-based national intelligence reconnaissance systems, consistent with the national security, it is hereby ordered as follows:

Section 1. Public Release of Historical Intelligence Imagery. Imagery acquired by the space-based national intelligence reconnaissance systems known as the Corona, Argon, and Lanyard missions shall, within 18 months of the date of this order, be declassified and transferred to the National Archives and Records Administration with a copy sent to the United States Geological Survey of the Department of the Interior consistent with procedures approved by the Director of Central Intelligence and the Archivist of the United States. Upon transfer, such imagery shall be deemed declassified and shall be made available to the public.

Sec. 2. Review for Future Public Release of Intelligence Imagery. (a) All information that meets the criteria in section 2(b) of this order shall be kept secret in the interests of national defense and foreign policy until deemed otherwise by the Director of Central Intelligence. In consultation with the Secretaries of State and Defense, the Director of Central Intelligence shall establish a comprehensive program for the periodic review of imagery from systems other than the Corona, Argon, and Lanyard missions, with the objective of making available to the public as much imagery as possible consistent with the interests of national defense and foreign policy. For imagery from obsolete broad-area film-return systems other than Corona, Argon, and Lanyard missions, this review shall be completed within 5 years of the date of this order. Review of imagery from any other system that the Director of Central Intelligence deems to be obsolete shall be accomplished according to a timetable established by the Director of Central Intelligence. The Director of Central Intelligence shall report annually to the President on the implementation of this order.

(b) The criteria referred to in section 2(a) of this order consist of the following: imagery acquired by a space-based national intelligence reconnaissance system other than the Corona, Argon, and Lanyard missions.

Sec. 3. General Provisions. (a) This order prescribes a comprehensive and exclusive system for the public release of imagery acquired by space-based national intelligence reconnaissance systems. This order is the exclusive Executive order governing the public release of imagery for purposes of section 552(b)(1) of the Freedom of Information Act.

(b) Nothing contained in this order shall create any right or benefit, substantive or procedural, enforceable by any party against the United States, its agencies or instrumentalities, its officers or employees, or any other person.

Sec. 4. Definition. As used herein, "imagery" means the product acquired by space-based national intelligence reconnaissance systems that provides a likeness or representation of any natural or man-made feature or related objective or activities and satellite positional data acquired at the same time the likeness or representation was acquired.

WILLIAM J. CLINTON

THE WHITE HOUSE,
February 22, 1995.

The most comprehensive available statement on intelligence community interest in environmental issues is a July 25, 1996 speech
before the World Affairs Council in Los Angeles by DCI John Deutch.
The speech, reprinted below, covered activities of the Environmental
Task Force and MEDEA, as well as the U.S.-Russia environmental
cooperation involving the exchange of intelligence data.

Public Affairs
S T A F F

DCI Speech 07/25/96

DCI Speech at the World Affairs Council in Los Angeles, California

"The Environment on the Intelligence Agenda"

The environment is an important part of the Intelligence Community agenda. Today I would like to explain
what we mean by the term 'environmental intelligence,' why the Intelligence Community is involved in this
work, and why our involvement is important for citizens of the United States and the world. I also want to
demonstrate that environmental intelligence is not a new or expensive area of endeavor for the Intelligence
Community.

****

The Intelligence Community's job is to ensure that our senior policymakers and military commanders have
objective information that will allow them to make better decisions. Through our collection and analytic effort,
we compile intelligence reports that give our country's leadership insight into how events in all parts of the
world will unfold and how these events will affect our national security.

Environmental trends, both natural and man-made, are among the underlying forces that affect a nation's
economy, its social stability, its behavior in world markets, and its attitude toward neighbors.

I emphasize that environment is one factor. It would be foolish, for example, to attribute conflicts in Somalia,
Ethiopia, or Haiti to environmental causes alone. It would be foolhardy, however, not to take into
consideration that the land in each of these states is exploited in a manner that can no longer support growing
populations.

Environmental degradation, encroaching deserts, erosion, and overfarming destroy vast tracts of arable land.
This forces people from their homes and creates tensions between ethnic and political groups as competition
for scarce resources increases. There is an essential connection between environmental degradation, population
growth, and poverty that regional analysts must take into account.

National reconnaissance systems that track the movement of tanks through the desert, can, at the same time,
track the movement of the desert itself, see the sand closing in on formerly productive fields or hillsides laid
bare by deforestation and erosion. Satellite systems allow us to quickly assess the magnitude and severity of
damage. Adding this environmental dimension to traditional political, economic, and military analysis enhances
our ability to alert policymakers to potential instability, conflict, or human disaster and to identify situations
which may draw in American involvement.

Some events have already dictated that environmental issues be included in our intelligence agenda. When
Moscow initially issued misleading information about the accident at the Chernobyl Nuclear Power Plant, US
leaders turned to the Intelligence Community to assess the damage and its impact on the former Soviet Union
and neighboring countries.

During the Gulf War, when Saddam Hussein used ecological destruction as a weapon, policymakers and the military called on the Intelligence Community to track the movement of smoke from burning oilfields and the flow of oil released into the gulf. They asked whether damage to Iraq's Tuwaitha nuclear complex posed a danger to troops and local population.

In each of these cases, our answer to these questions was not and could not be, "the environment is not an intelligence issue." Our answers were classic intelligence: analysis based on our data from collection systems and open sources. We were able to assess the magnitude of the Chernobyl accident; we were able to tell US troops how to avoid lethal hydrogen sulfide from oil fires; and we were able to tell military planners that damage to the reactor was not a threat.

I would like to emphasize that the environment is not a new issue for the Intelligence Community. For years we have devoted resources to understanding environmental issues. Much of the work that now falls under the environmental label used to be done under other names--geography, resource issues, or research.

For example, we have long used satellite imagery to estimate crop size in North Korea and elsewhere. This allowed us to forecast shortages that might lead to instability and to determine the amount of agricultural products a nation would need to import--information valuable to US Department of Agriculture and to America's farmers. We have also tracked world availability of natural resources, such as oil, gas, and minerals.

We have for many years provided the military with information on terrain and local resources. As our forces embark on military, peacekeeping, and humanitarian operations in remote and unfamiliar territory, they will need even better information on environmental factors that could affect their health and safety and their ability to conduct operations.

Diplomacy will be ever more concerned with the global debate over environmental issues. As Secretary of State Christopher said in April, "our ability to advance our global interests is inextricably linked to how we manage the Earth's natural resources." He emphasized that we must put environment "in the mainstream of American foreign policy."

Intelligence has long supported diplomacy in this area, particularly in regard to key international environmental treaties and agreements. Here I would draw an analogy to the role of intelligence in negotiating the arms control treaties. Such treaties could not have been signed and ratified without intelligence to monitor compliance.

Likewise, the Intelligence Community monitors compliance with environmental treaties, such as the Montreal Protocol on Substances that Deplete the Stratospheric Ozone Layer and the London Convention that regulates the dumping at sea of radioactive and other wastes. Further, intelligence support should begin with the negotiation process, so that US diplomats have the benefit of the best available information in framing effective and enforceable treaties in the future.

Environmental intelligence will also be a part of our support to economic policymakers. They need to know, for example, whether or not foreign competitors are gaining a competitive advantage over American business by ignoring environmental regulations. Intelligence can provide valuable information.

In short, the demand on the Intelligence Community for information on environmental issues will grow. As the world population expands and resources such as clean water and arable land become more scarce, it will become increasingly likely that activities of one country will have an environmental impact that goes beyond its borders. US policymakers will need warning on issues that are likely to affect US interests and regional stability.

Maintaining a capability for environmental intelligence will allow us to answer important questions that are likely to come from our consumers in the future. For example, China's rapidly growing population and booming economy will translate into a tremendous increase in demand for the world's natural resources, including oil and food. What impact will this have on world markets? As in the past, we must be prepared to answer such questions.

We should also be willing to provide data from our collection systems to help experts answer less traditional questions, for example: what impact will increased burning of fossil fuel have on the global environment?

****

As I have mentioned, the Intelligence Community has unique assets, including satellites, sensors, and remote sensing expertise that can contribute a wealth of information on the environment to the scientific community. We also have mechanisms in place to share that information with outside experts. This effort will add significantly to our nation's capability to anticipate environmental crises.

In 1991, then-Senator Gore urged the Intelligence Community to create a task force to explore ways that intelligence assets could be tapped to support environmental research. That initiative led to a partnership between the Intelligence and scientific communities that has proven to be extraordinarily productive for both parties.

The Environmental Task Force found that data collected by the Intelligence Community from satellites and other means can fill critical information gaps for the environmental science community. Furthermore, these data can be handed over for study without revealing information about sources and methods.

For example, imagery from the earliest intelligence satellites--which were launched long before commercial systems--can show scientists how desert boundaries, vegetation, and polar ice have changed over time. These historical images, which have now been declassified, provide valuable indicators of regional and global climate change.

Some of the scientists who participated in the Environmental Task force now make up a group called MEDEA. MEDEA works with the Intelligence Community to establish what we call the "Global Fiducials Program." Under this initiative, during the next decade we will periodically image selected sites of environmental significance. This will give scientists an ongoing record of changes in the earth that will improve their understanding of environmental processes. More importantly, it will greatly enhance their ability to provide strategic warning of potentially catastrophic threats to the health and welfare of our citizens.

At the same time, we do not see the Intelligence Community becoming a center of environmental science expertise or directly sponsoring research in that area. In this case, our job is to acquire the data and allow the scientific community to use them. Their work, quite properly, is sponsored by others, such as the National Science Foundation, the National Oceanic and Atmospheric Administration, National Aeronautics and Space Administration and academic institutions. We will continue to work with environmental experts to assure that their knowledge is brought to bear on what data we collect or retrieve from our considerable archives.

Our interaction with MEDEA is not only valuable for the environmental community, it also has had direct benefits for the Intelligence Community. MEDEA has worked closely with our analysts to develop techniques that have enhanced our ability to collect and interpret data from our collection systems.

Combining Intelligence Community data and expertise with knowledge from the scientific community can produce a better intelligence product for policymakers. Scientists from MEDEA worked with our analysts to respond to requests for information on environmental issues and problems--such as a series of oil spills in the Komi region of Russia. The Komi oil spill is just one example of how intelligence satellites and sensors can provide valuable information quickly after a natural or man-made disaster. In this case we could tell that large amounts of oil were not getting into the Arctic rivers.

In the United States, the Intelligence Community provides support to the Federal Emergency Management Agency and other civil agencies when there is a natural disaster. Using data from a variety of sources, within hours after a disaster strikes we can assess and report the nature and scope of the damage -- conditions of roads, airports and hospitals; and the status of potential secondary threats such as dams and nuclear facilities. Here I would like to make two points:

- First, we only provide this support upon request. To image US territory, we must first get permission.

- Second, we provide unclassified products generated from classified information. We have a Disaster Response Team that can quickly produce unclassified maps and diagrams that show the damage resulting from an earthquake, fire, flood, hurricane, oil spill, or volcanic eruption.

To give you a recent example of how well this system works, just a few weeks ago (June 5), the US Forest Service requested our help in tracking the wildfires raging in Alaska. In this instance, they did not have enough planes to adequately chart the extent of the fires. Within 24 hours of the initial request, we delivered a map depicting the fire perimeter, smoldering fires, and the most intense blazes. This information was more comprehensive and detailed than data collected from overflights by civil aircraft and it was also available much more quickly than would have otherwise been possible.

We can also use our capabilities to provide warning before a disaster strikes. And we do share this information with foreign governments. For example, when a volcano on the Caribbean Island of Montserrat awakened in 1995, we monitored significant changes and alerted U.S. and British West Indies aid and military authorities so that they could prepare for a possible evacuation of the island's residents. Recently we noted a change within the volcano crater--a fissure had opened up, indicating that the risk of an eruption had increased dramatically. We quickly sent out a warning that allowed authorities on Montserrat to evacuate 4,000 people to a less dangerous area of the island.

These activities lie outside our traditional intelligence mission, but we believe it is important to provide aid when the capabilities would not otherwise be available. This effort costs us very little, and yields tremendous benefits to relief agencies, disaster victims, and potential victims whose lives could be saved by a timely warning.

****

Vice President Gore has been a leader in advocating the use of intelligence information to improve environmental knowledge on an international level, for example to better monitor oil spills and chemical waste streams through international water ways.

The US-Russian Joint Commission on Economic and Technological Cooperation--the Gore-Chernomyrdin Commission--has established a productive exchange of information between the US and Russia.

This exchange has brought us unique and valuable data from Russia's intelligence programs. For example, the Russians have collected extensive data on the Arctic Ocean. This information is critical to our understanding of oceanographic and atmospheric processes, which are, in turn, critical to our ability to predict global climate change. Together with Russia, we have produced a CD-ROM atlas of the Arctic Ocean. It contains more than two million individual observations collected from 1948 to 1993 by Russian drifting stations, ice breakers, and airborne expeditions, as well as observations from US buoys. This once-restricted data will now be available on the Internet through the World Wide Web and will more than double the scientific holdings of oceanographic data available to US scientists.

The Arctic data are not only critical to scientific studies of climate change. They can also help us chart the movement of pollutants. The great rivers of Russia flow north into the Arctic. With them, they carry a heavy burden of waste from Russian industry, including chemicals, heavy metals, and organics, as well as radionuclides from Russia's defense programs. For example, 3 million curies of radioactive waste from Chelyabinsk , dumped into the Techa River years ago, have migrated to the Arctic Ocean, over 1,500 kilometers from the plant. Russian oceanographic data can help them and us to determine where radioactive materials and pollutants will travel once they reach the Arctic and whether they will affect US and Canadian waters.

Early this year, Russia and the United States exchanged declassified imagery-derived diagrams of environmental damage over a 25-year period at Eglin Air Force Base in Florida and Yeysk Airbase in southwestern Russia. This ongoing exchange will help both countries clean up their toxic and radioactive sites. The techniques used to create these maps could help us identify potential sources of contamination in the future. Such information-sharing has proven a low-cost and highly effective way to build good will and strengthen international relationships. We should seek new opportunities to share information with other countries.

****

I would like to make one more key point about our work on environmental issues--the costs are small and the potential benefits enormous. The resources allocated to environmental intelligence are modest, perhaps one tenth of a percent of the intelligence budget for collection and analysis. We are using intelligence capabilities that are already in place. This important work requires no new capital investments.

Nor does environmental intelligence require us to divert collection systems from our priority targets or get involved in areas where we do not belong. The imaging of sites under the Global Fiducials program, for example, can be done during non-peak hours of satellite use. It will not interfere with collection against our highest priority targets, including the proliferation of weapons of mass destruction, terrorism, drug trafficking, and the activities of rogue states.

****

In sum, the environment will continue to have an important place on the US intelligence agenda.

- Environmental factors influence the internal and external political, economic, and military actions of nations important to our national security.
- Our intelligence customers, including the policy and military communities, need--and ask for--support on environmental issues and problems.
- The Intelligence Community has unique technical collection resources and analytic expertise that can fill critical information gaps for environmental scientists or help relief agencies cope with natural disasters.
- Through a productive partnership with the scientific community, we can provide strategic warning of environmental hazards that could endanger our health and welfare.
- These activities do not threaten our traditional missions.
- The vital work I have described requires only a modest commitment of resources.

I think it would be short-sighted for us to ignore environmental issues as we seek to understand and forecast developments in the post-Cold War world and identify threats to our national welfare. Just as Secretary Christopher promised "to put environmental issues in the mainstream of American Foreign policy," I intend to make sure that Environmental Intelligence remains in the mainstream of US intelligence activities. Even in times of declining budgets we will support policymakers and the military as they address these important environmental issues.

[CIA Home Page]

Books and Reports

Bridge to a Sustainable Future: National Environmental Technology Strategy, Government Printing Office, Washington, D.C., April 1995.

Commercial Observation Satellites and International Security, Michael Krepon, Peter D. Zimmerman, Leonard S. Spector, and Mary Umberger (eds.), St. Martin's Press, New York, 1990.

Emerging Markets of the Information Age: A Case Study in Remote Sensing Data and Technology, C. B. Gabbard, K. O'Connell, G. Park, P.J.E. Stan, RAND, DB-176-CIRA, 1996.

The Future of Remote Sensing from Space: Civilian Satellite Systems and Applications, U.S. Congress, Office of Technology Assessment, OTA-ISC-558, U.S. Government Printing Office, Washington, D.C., 1993.

IC21: Intelligence Community in the 21st Century, Staff Study, Permanent Select Committee on Intelligence, U.S. House of Representatives, One Hundred Fourth Congress, U.S. Government Printing Office, Washington, D.C., April 9, 1996.

The Interior Budget in Brief for FY97, U.S. Geological Survey—Bureau Summary, U.S. Department of the Interior, U.S. Government Printing Office, Washington, D.C., March 1996.

New Satellite Images for Sale, the Opportunities and Risks Ahead, Vipin Gupta, Lawrence Livermore National Laboratory, Center for Security and Technology Studies, CSTS-47-94, Livermore, California, September 28, 1994.

1995 MTPE/EOS Reference Handbook, NASA, Washington, D.C., available on the World Wide Web at http://spso.gsfc.nasa.gov/ eos_reference/TOC.html

Preparing for the Future Through Science and Technology: An Agenda for Environmental and Natural Resource Research, National Science and Technology Council, Committee on Environment and Natural Resources, Washington, D.C., March 1995.

Preparing for the 21st Century: An Appraisal of U.S. Intelligence, Report of the Commission on the Roles and Capabilities of the United States Intelligence Community, U.S. Government Printing Office, Washington, D.C., March 1, 1996.

Redefining Security: A Report of the Joint Security Commission, a report to the Secretary of Defense and the Director, Central Intelligence, Washington, D.C., February 28, 1994.

Rubenson, D., M. D. Millot, G. Farnsworth, and J. Aroesty, *More Than 25 Million Acres? DoD as a Federal, Natural, and Cultural Resource Manager,* RAND, MR-715-OSD, 1996.

Scientific Utility of Naval Environmental Data, a MEDEA Special Task Force Report, Washington, D.C., June 1995.

Stability Implications of Open-Market Availability of Space-Based Sensor and Navigation Information, final report, Science Applications International Corporation, McLean, Virginia, November 9, 1995.

Periodicals

"Ancient Sea-level Swings Confirmed," Richard A. Kerr, *Science,* Vol. 272, No. 5265, May 24, 1996, pp. 1097–1098.

"The Art and Science of Photoreconnaissance," Dino A. Brugioni, *Scientific American,* March 1996, pp. 78–85.

"California Social Climbers: Low Water Prompts High Status," Joshua Fischman, *Science*, May 10, 1996, pp. 811–812.

"CIA Discloses Disaster Monitoring with National Space Systems," Associated Press, October 20, 1995.

"Imagery, Mapping Agency's Client Focus Drives Agility," Clarence A. Robinson, Jr., *Signal*, April 1996, pp. 39–42.

"Lockheed Martin to Purchase Hughes Share of EOSAT," Lockheed Martin Missiles & Space Press Release 96-32, Sunnyvale, California, June 7, 1996.

"Navy Is Releasing Treasure of Secret Data on World's Oceans," William J. Broad, *New York Times*, November 28, 1995, p. C-1.

"New Image of Seafloor Has Broad Applications," Reuters, October 23, 1995.

"NRO Images Available to the Public, But Early Use Is Light," *Space Business News*, May 15, 1996, p. 8.

"Russia, U.S. Swap Images to Clean Up Bases," UPI, April 22, 1996.

"Russian Spy Satellites to Save United States from Earthquakes and Greenhouse Effect," Leonid Mlechin, *Izvestiya*, July 22, 1995, p. 3.

"Some Current International and National Earth Observation Data Policies," Ray Harris, Roman Krawec, *Space Policy*, November 1993, pp. 273–285.

"Spying on the Environment," Robert Dreyfuss, *"E"–the Environmental Magazine*, January/February 1995.

TODAY: America's Forces Protect the Environment, DoD Legacy Resource Management Program, project magazine, Washington, D.C., 1995.

"Tortoises Get Some Unusual Help from the Military's Spy Satellites," *New York Times*, May 14, 1996, p. C-4.

"Tracking a Dwindling Desert Denizen," *Washington Post*, March 18, 1996, A, 3:1.

"U.S.-Soviet Spy Imagery Exchange Aids Environment," *Space News*, February 12–18, 1996, p. 18.

"U.S. Will Deploy Its Spy Satellites on Nature Mission," William J. Broad, *New York Times*, November 27, 1995, p. A-1.

Conference Proceedings, Briefings, and Speeches

"American Diplomacy and the Global Environmental Challenges of the 21st Century," Secretary of State Warren Christopher, Palo Alto, California, April 9, 1996.

"Environmental Program," briefing, Central Intelligence Agency, Fall 1995.

"Federal Government Market for High Resolution Panchromatic Imagery," briefing, KPMG Peat Marwick, April 7, 1995.

"Gore-Chernomyrdin Environmental Working Group—Project Summary," briefing, January 1996.

"Information Sharing Initiative with the Russian Government," Dr. Ashton Carter, Assistant Secretary of Defense (International Security Policy), DoD News Briefing, Defenselink Transcript, January 31, 1996.

"Pan-Pacific Hazards '96—A Conference on Earthquakes, Volcanoes, and Tsunamis," conference abstracts, Vancouver, British Columbia, Canada, July 29–August 2, 1996.

Legislation, Government Policy, Agreements and Statements

Classification of National Security Information, Executive Order 12958, Washington, D.C., April 20, 1995.

Governing Intelligence Activities (excerpts), Executive Order 12333, Washington, D.C., December 4, 1981.

"Memorandum Between the Department of Defense of the United States of America and the Ministry of Defense of the Russian Federation on Cooperation in Environmental Protection Issues," Moscow, Russia, June 30, 1995.

"A National Security Strategy of Engagement and Enlargement," The White House, Washington, D.C., July 1994.

"Paperwork Reduction Act of 1995, Section 2. Coordination of Federal Information Policy," P.L. 104-13, May 22, 1995.

Office of Management and Budget, Circular No. A-11, *Preparation and Submission of Budget Estimates*, June 13, 1996.

————, Circular No. A-130, *Management of Federal Information Resources* (revised), February 8, 1996.

————, Circular No. A-76, *Performance of Commercial Activities*, August 3, 1983.

Omnibus Civilian Science Authorization Act of 1996, Committee on Science Report Together with Dissenting Views, U.S. House of Representatives, One Hundred Fourth Congress, Report 104-550, Washington, D.C., May 1, 1996.

Policy on Foreign Access to Remote Sensing Space Capabilities, Fact Sheet, U.S. Department of Commerce, March 10, 1994.

Release of Imagery Acquired by Space-Based National Intelligence Reconnaissance Systems, Executive Order 12951, Washington, D.C., February 22, 1995.